ALFRED ADLER

Co-operation Between the Sexes

Writings on Women and Men, Love and Marriage, and Sexuality

EDITED AND TRANSLATED BY

HEINZ L. ANSBACHER AND

ROWENA R. ANSBACHER

WITH AN ESSAY BY HEINZ L. ANSBACHER

W. W. NORTON & COMPANY, INC.
NEW YORK • LONDON

Heinz L. Ansbacher, Professor Emeritus of psychology at the University of Vermont, has contributed numerous symposium chapters and encyclopedia articles on Alfred Adler, and edited Adler's *The Science of Living.* Rowena R. Ansbacher, his wife, has been his long-time associate as former editor of the *Journal of Individual Psychology.* Together, the Ansbachers have edited two books of Adler's writings, *The Individual Psychology of Alfred Adler* and *Superiority and Social Interest.*

Printed in the United States of America.

First published as a Norton paperback 1982 by arrangement with Doubleday & Company, Inc.

W. W. Norton & Company, Inc., 500 Fifth Avenue, New York, NY 10110
W. W. Norton & Company Ltd, 10 Coptic Street, London WC1A 1PU

3 4 5 6 7 8 9 0

ISBN 0-393-30019-6

CONTENTS

PREFACE

The theory of sexuality of Alfred Adler (1870–1937) is best characterized as the opposite of Freud's. Whereas Freud believed a person's sexuality determines his personality, Adler asserted that the total personality, the style of life, determines the sexuality.

The purpose of the present book is to gather Adler's writings on sex and related matters such as feminism, love, and marriage in one volume so that they can be examined as a whole.

Such a volume seems to be particularly called for at this time of heightened interest in sex and widespread rejection of Freud's theories, from members of women's liberation movements to psychoanalysts.

Adler considered sex one of the three great life problems every human being must meet, the others being work and social relations. Since Adler, furthermore, emphasized the unity of the personality, a presentation of his sexual theories will be practically an introduction to his theory of personality as a whole.

The book is arranged in four chapters, forming two parts. Part I, "Sociological and Theoretical Writings," presents in Chapter 1 Adler's views on the "woman question," which are strongly on the side of equality of the sexes. They most likely preceded Adler's psychological work, although they were not published in that order. Chapter 2 is the first full-length translation of Adler's critique of Freud's theory of sexuality, augmented by some further early theoretical writing.

Part II, "Sexuality and the Individual," deals in Chapter 3

with sexual development, women's and men's psychosexual attitudes, and sex education and puberty. Chapter 4 deals at length with problems of love and marriage, including reasons for disturbances, and the dynamics involved in preparation for love and marriage.

A third section, "Sexual Disorders," has been omitted from the Norton edition. (The complete edition is published in cloth by Jason Aronson.)

Since the material for this volume was gathered from many different sources, some overlapping was unavoidable, and there is also a certain unevenness of style. Some parts, written for the general public as they were, offer relatively easy reading, while others were addressed to more or less specialized professional readers.

A word regarding terminology is also indicated. Two terms most widely identified with Adler's psychology, "social interest" and "life style," appear relatively infrequently, although equivalents for "life style"—expressing the personality as a whole—are found throughout. These two terms were not introduced by Adler until 1918 and 1926, respectively, while most of his writings on the present subject matter were composed earlier. On the other hand, the term "masculine protest," which figures so large in these early writings, was later replaced by such concepts as striving for success, power, superiority, or simply a plus situation.

A great part of the material is here translated for the first time or retranslated, as indicated by footnotes to the various sections. Also, nearly all the headings and subheadings have been supplied by the editors.

An "Essay" by the first editor follows Adler's writings. Section 3, "The Masculine Protest," deals with the quite technical theoretical issues involved in Chapter 2.

The present volume must be considered the last of a trilogy. The first, *The Individual Psychology of Alfred Adler* (New York: Basic Books, 1956; Harper Torch Books, 1964) is a systematic presentation of Adler's work in selections from all his writings. The second, *Superiority and Social Interest* (Evanston, Ill.: Northwestern University Press, 1964; 3rd ed., New York: W. W. Norton, 1979) is a collection of later writings presented in full length, and includes a biographical essay by Carl Furtmüller as well as a complete Adler bibliography.

* * *

Initial translation of most of Chapter 3 and the first two sections of Chapter 4 was supported by Public Health Service Research Grant No. MH-14330–01 from the National Institute of Mental Health. In this connection I wish to express sincere and lasting gratitude to my colleague at the University of Vermont, Donald G. Forgays, at that time chairman of the Department of Psychology. It was he who got me started on this book by encouraging my grant application and helping it along. He has always been a good personal friend, as well as a friend and supporter of Adlerian psychology.

Continued deep gratitude goes to my wife, Rowena R. Ansbacher, co-editor of the present volume as well as the two preceding. She gave particularly valuable help in selecting some of the material for inclusion and going over much of the translation.

I am very grateful to the faithful coworkers I had in typing—Sherrill Musty, who took down the first translations, Leslie Weiger, who was most helpful and supportive in the middle stages, and Hildegarde Bolsterle, who saw the manuscript through to a happy ending.

To return to Adler, he saw the solution to all of life's problems in rational co-operative effort among equals who, as responsible fellow human beings and respecting each other, would strive independently and interdependently toward commonly useful goals. He gained this perspective from his convictions and observations on psychological patients and embodied it in a theory which he took great pains to place on a scientifically sound foundation which adhered to the realities of life as closely as possible.

The particular message of the present book is that the life problem of sex and marriage is not to be solved on an individual basis—if humanity and in turn each individual is to benefit, even survive. As we are completing this book, we note a rising storm of voices pronouncing that such a message has become increasingly urgent. Adler saw the solution in a close co-operation between two individuals of different sex, committed not to a mistaken "self-actualization" but an actualization of each other and, through children, the future of humanity. Hence the main title of the present collection: *Co-operation Between the Sexes.*

HEINZ L. ANSBACHER

University of Vermont
Burlington, Vermont
February 27, 1978

PART I

Sociological and Theoretical Writings

1

THE MYTH OF WOMEN'S INFERIORITY[1]

DIVISION OF LABOR AND SEXUAL DIMORPHISM[2]

The two factors that dominate all psychological processes are social interest (*Gemeinschaftsgefühl*) and striving for significance (*Geltungsstreben*). In constructing and securing the conditions of his life, in meeting the three main tasks of life—love, occupation, society—man always activates his social interest and effects his striving for significance, for power, and for superiority. Any psychological phenomenon must be evaluated by the quantitative and qualitative relationship of these two factors to each other to approximate a psychological understanding. The relationship of these factors will determine the extent to which a person will be capable of comprehending the logic of human living together, and of adapting himself to the division of labor that this logic enforces.

Division of labor is an absolute necessity for the preservation of human society. Consequently, every person must fill a specific place at some point. If a person does not participate in fulfilling this obligation, he denies the preservation of so-

[1] New translation of A1927a, Part 1, Chap. 7, *Das Verhältnis der Geschlechter* (The Relationship of the Sexes), except for the last two sections.

[2] A1927a, pp. 95–97.

cial life, of the human race altogether. He forgets his role as a fellow man and becomes a troublemaker. In lighter such cases we speak of bad manners, mischief, doing things your own way; in more difficult cases, of eccentricity, delinquency; and in later life, of crime. Such phenomena are condemned exclusively on account of their distance from and incompatibility with the demands of social life.

A person's worth is determined by how he fills the place that is assigned to him in the division of labor of the community. In his affirmation of the social life he becomes significant for others, and one of the links of a thousandfold chain on which the continuation of human life is based, and in which the absence of a certain number of these links would result in the collapse of social life. Ideally, it will be the individual's abilities that will assign to him his place in the total production process of human society. But quite some confusion has crept into this understanding and has disturbed the division of labor on this basis by setting false criteria for the evaluation of human worth. An individual may for some reason be unsuited for the place in which he finds himself; or difficulties may have arisen from the power craving or false ambition of certain individuals who in their own egotistical interest impede this kind of human living together and working together. Personal power or economic interests cause work to be distributed so that the more enjoyable positions, which give more power, are attained by certain groups of society, whereas others are excluded from them. Since the striving for power plays an enormous role in these matters, the process of division of labor never took place smoothly. Continuous violent intervention has rendered work a kind of privilege for some, and a kind of oppression for others.

Such a division of labor is also given through human sexual dimorphism [*Zweigeschlechtlichkeit* (division into two sexes)]. From the start this excludes one part, the female, from certain occupations according to her physique, while other jobs are not assigned to men because they can be employed better elsewhere. This division of labor should be carried through according to a completely unprejudiced criterion.

The woman's movement, insofar as it does not overdo things in the heat of battle, has accepted the logic of this viewpoint. It does not defeminize women nor destroy the natural relations of man and woman toward the work opportunities suited for them. In the course of human development the division of labor took the form that the woman takes over a part of those jobs that otherwise would also keep the man busy, while the latter can employ his powers more usefully. This division of labor is not quite unreasonable as long as labor resources are not thereby rendered idle and intellectual and physical resources are misused.

THE CULTURAL SITUATION

Male Dominance[3]

Through the development of culture in the direction of the striving for power, especially through the efforts of certain individuals or classes who wanted to secure privileges for themselves, the division of labor has been steered in favor of the men. This trend prevails to this day, with the result that human culture is characterized by the overtowering significance of man. The division of labor is such that the men are the group with guaranteed privileges. Due to their dominance, men influence the female position in the division of labor, in the production process, to their own advantage. Men prescribe to women their sphere of life and are in a position to enforce this; they determine forms of life for women that follow primarily the male viewpoint.

As matters stand today, men continuously strive for superiority over women, while women are constantly dissatisfied with the male privileges. Since, however, the two sexes belong closely together, there is tension, a constant upset of psychological harmony. This general psychological condition is experienced as extremely painful by both parts of the human race and leads to far-reaching disturbances.

[3] A1927a, pp. 97–100, with some omissions, covered later.

Male dominance did not originate as a natural fact, but had to be secured by a number of laws. Before that, there must have been periods when male dominance was not so certain. There is indeed historical evidence for a time of matriarchy, matrilineality (*Mutterrecht*), when the mother, the woman, played the more important role in life, especially toward the child, and all men of the tribe had a kind of obligation to her. Certain customs and traditions still point to this, as for example the usage of jokingly referring to every man as a child's uncle or cousin.

The transition from matriarchy to patriarchy was preceded by a great battle. Originally man did indeed not have the privileges that today he likes to describe as due him by nature, but had to fight for them. A good detailed description of this development is to be found in August Bebel (1885), *Woman and Socialism*. The victory of the men was tantamount to the subjugation of the women. Especially the records of the development of law testify eloquently to this process of subjugation.

Male dominance has not been a natural state, but became necessary only in the course of continuous fighting with neighboring peoples, when a significant role fell to man that he finally used to seize leadership definitely. Hand in hand with this went the development of private property and the law of inheritance as a foundation of male predominance, inasmuch as man is generally the earning and owning part.

The View of Women's Inferiority[4]

To justify his dominance, man generally argues that, in addition to his position being due him by nature, woman is an inferior being. The view of women's inferiority is so widespread that it appears as if it were common to all human beings. Together with this, a certain unrest is found in man, which probably stems from the time of the struggle against matriarchy, when woman indeed represented a disquieting factor for man.

[4] A1927a, pp. 103–7, with some omissions, covered later.

In history and literature we continually meet hints of this kind. Thus a Roman writer says, *"Mulier est hominis confusio."* [Woman is the confusion of man.] At Church councils the question of whether woman had a soul was the object of lively discussion, and learned treatises were written on the question of whether she was a human being at all. Witch hunting, with its witch burnings, lasted for centuries, and is sad testimony to the errors, to the enormous insecurity and confusion at that time, regarding this question.

Women often are presented as the cause of all evil in the world, as in the Bible story of original sin, or in Homer's *Iliad,* in which one woman was sufficient to plunge entire peoples into misery. Legends and fairy tales of all times refer to the moral inferiority of women, their depravity, malice, deceitfulness, fickleness, and unreliability. "Female frivolity" is even mentioned in support of laws. Similarly, women are depreciated regarding competence and performance. Figures of speech, anecdotes, proverbs, and jokes of all peoples are full of depreciating criticism of women. They are accused of quarrelsomeness, unpunctuality, pettiness, and stupidity.

Extraordinary acuity is mustered to prove woman's inferiority, to think only of persons such as Strindberg, Moebius, Schopenhauer, and Weininger. Their number is enlarged by many women who, in their resignation, came to share the view of woman's inferiority and her deserved subordinate role. The low esteem of women is also expressed in far lower pay for women than for men, even when their work is equal in value to men's work.

It is true that aptitude tests have shown that in certain subjects, such as mathematics, boys do better, and in other subjects, such as languages, girls do better. Boys show indeed more aptitude than girls for subjects that prepare for male occupations. But this speaks only apparently for their greater aptitude. If one looks more closely at the situation of girls, it turns out that the story of the lesser ability of women is a fable, a lie, which only looks like a truth.

A further argument against the prejudice of women's inferiority is the substantial number of women who have become outstanding in the most varied fields, especially literature, art, technology, and medicine, whose accomplishments fully equal those of men. Incidentally, the number of men who show no accomplishments but a high degree of incompetence is so great that one could defend with an equal mass of evidence a myth of the inferiority of men—of course equally unjustly.

A serious result of this myth of the inferiority of everything female is a peculiar dichotomy of concepts. Masculine is simply identified with valuable, strong, and victorious, and feminine with obedient, servile, and subordinated. This manner of thinking has become so deeply rooted in our culture that everything excellent has a male tint, whereas everything that is less valuable and objectionable is represented as feminine. As is well known, for some men the worst insult is, "just like a woman," whereas in girls manliness does not mean derogation. The accent is always placed so that everything that reminds one of the female is represented as inferior.

Phenomena that frequently support this myth so clearly are upon closer observation nothing but the consequences of impeded development. We do not wish to claim that we could make of every child a person who in the usual sense can be considered "gifted" or very able. But we are confident that we could make of every child a person who would be considered *untalented*. We have of course never done this, but we know that others have succeeded in doing so. And it is very plausible that this is today more often the fate of girls than of boys. We have had occasion to see such "untalented" children who one day appeared so gifted that it seemed as if they had virtually been transformed.

EFFECTS ON THE CHILDREN

Boys[5]

All our institutions, traditions, laws, morals, and customs bear witness to the privileged position of the male toward whom they are oriented and by whom they are maintained.

[5] A1927a, pp. 98–103.

They penetrate as far as the nursery and have an enormous influence on the child's psyche. Though we cannot assume that the understanding of the child for these coherences is great, the child is sensitive to them. Consider the case of a boy who answered the demand to put on girl's clothing with a vehement temper tantrum. Such occurrences give us enough reason to investigate these coherences. This leads us again, from another side, to a consideration of the striving for power.

Once the boy's striving for significance has reached a certain degree, he will prefer to take the path that appears guaranteed by the privileges of his masculinity, which he sees everywhere. Present-day family education is very well suited to advance the striving for power and thereby the inclination to value male privileges highly and to aspire to them. The reason is that usually the man, the father, confronts the child as a symbol of power. By his mysterious comings and goings he arouses the child's interest much more than does the mother.

Very soon the child notices the overtowering role that the father takes; he sets the tone, makes arrangements, directs everything. The child sees how everybody defers to his orders and how the mother constantly refers to him. In every respect man appears to the child as the strong and powerful one. To some children the father appears so authoritative that they believe whatever he says must be holy, and in order to strengthen an assertion often reply only, "Father said so."

Even where the father's influence is not so clearly apparent, children will get the impression that the father is superior, because the entire burden of the family seems to rest on him, whereas actually only the division of labor gives the father the opportunity to employ his resources better.

The growing child does not need to read books on the subject. Even if he knows nothing of these matters, he will feel the result of the fact that man is the earning and privileged part, even when sensible fathers and mothers are gladly willing to renounce these old traditional privileges in favor of equal rights. It is extremely difficult to explain to a child that the mother, who performs the domestic work, is a partner who has equal rights with the father.

Imagine what it must mean for a boy to see before him from his first day everywhere the priority of man. Already at birth he is received much more joyfully than a little girl, and is celebrated as a prince. Everybody knows that all too frequently parents would rather have boys. The boy senses at every step how, as male progeny, he is preferred and considered more valuable. Various words addressed to him or occasionally picked up by him again and again suggest to him the greater importance of the masculine role.

The superiority of the masculine principle confronts a boy also in the form that the women living under the same roof with him are used for the less appreciated jobs, and finally that women in his environment are not always convinced of their equal value with men. They usually play a role that is presented as subordinated and inferior.

The child experiences all the situations that follow from this relationship. The result is innumerable pictures and opinions regarding the essence of woman, in which she generally emerges poorly. The psychological development of a boy thus receives a masculine cast. What he can sense as a desirable goal in his striving for power are almost exclusively masculine traits and attitudes.

From the described power relationships arises a sort of masculine virtue. Certain character traits that point to this origin are considered "masculine," others "feminine," without any basic facts justifying these valuations. When we compare boys and girls and find apparent confirmation of this classification, we cannot speak of natural facts. Rather, we note these phenomena in persons who are already tied to a certain frame, whose life plan, whose guiding line, is already narrowed down by one-sided power decisions. These power relationships have compellingly assigned to such persons the place on which they will have to seek their development.

The distinction of masculine and feminine character traits is thus not justified. We shall see that both kinds of traits can serve the demands of the striving for power, that one can exercise power also with "feminine" means—for example, through obedience and submission. Through the advantages that an obedient child enjoys, he may possibly move much more into the foreground than one who is disobedient, although in both cases the striving for power is at work. Our insight into a person is often made more difficult because the power striving resorts to the most varied character traits in order to prevail.

As a boy grows older, the significance of his masculinity almost becomes a duty. His ambition, his striving for power and superiority, are joined completely, become virtually identical with the obligation toward masculinity. Many children in their striving for power are not satisfied to carry the consciousness of masculinity merely within. They want always to show and prove that they are men and therefore must have privileges. On the one hand they try always to excel, and in doing so exaggerate their masculine character traits; on the other hand, they always try to demonstrate their superiority to the feminine environment, as all tyrants do, through defiance, or through tricky cunning, depending on the degree of resistance that they encounter.

Since every person is measured by the ideal of privileged masculinity, it is little wonder that this measure is always held up to a boy and that in the end he measures himself by it. He will ask himself and observe whether his bearing is always manly, whether he is already sufficiently manly, etc. All that is today presented as "manly" is familiar—first of all, something purely egotistical, something that satisfies self-love (that is, superiority), the pre-eminence over others—all this together with the help of active traits such as courage, strength, pride, memories of victories of all kinds (especially over women), the achievement of offices, honors, and titles, the inclination to harden oneself against "feminine" impulses, etc. It is a continuous struggle for personal superiority, because it is considered manly to be superior.

Thus a boy will adapt traits for which he can borrow the models only from adult men, especially his father. The traces of this artificially cultivated idea of grandeur can be followed everywhere. A boy is tempted early to secure for himself an excess of power and privileges. They mean to him as much as "manliness." In bad cases manliness often turns into the well-known phenomena of rudeness and brutality.

Girls[6]

The advantages that masculinity frequently offers are a great temptation, and thus many girls are guided by a masculine ideal. This may be expressed either as an unfulfillable yearning or as a criterion for the evaluation of their behavior, or as a manner of appearing and acting. "In matters of culture every woman will want to be a man." This includes the girls who in an indomitable urge prefer exactly those games and activities that according to physical aptitude would be more suitable for boys. They climb trees, like to move in the company of boys, and decline all feminine occupations as a disgrace. They find satisfaction only in masculine activity. All this is to be understood from the preference for masculinity. Here we see clearly how the struggle for an eminent position, the striving for superiority, extends more toward appearance than reality and the actual position in life.

A girl is told at every step, so to speak, daily, and in countless variations, that girls are incapable, and are suitable only for easier and subordinated work. Obviously, a little girl unable to examine such judgments for their correctness will regard female inability as woman's inevitable fate, and will ultimately herself believe in her own inability. Thereby discouraged, she does not meet such school subjects [as mathematics]—if she will ever have to do with them at all—with the necessary interest, or she loses interest in them. Thus she lacks external and internal preparation.

Under such circumstances the proof of woman's inability will of course seem correct. But it is an error for two reasons. The first reason is that the value of a person is still often judged on the basis of his performance from a business standpoint—that is, from a one-sided, purely self-seeking point of view. From this standpoint one can indeed overlook the question to what extent performance and aptitudes are connected with psychological development.

[6] A1927a, first paragraph, p. 103; the remainder, pp. 105–7.

The second and main reason is that from childhood a girl encounters a myth that is very likely to shake her belief in her own value, her self-confidence, and to undermine her hope of ever performing competently. When she is reinforced in this by seeing that women are assigned only subordinated roles, it is understandable that she will lose courage, will no longer want to take a real hold, and will eventually pull back from the tasks of life.

Then, of course, she is really unfit and useless. When we face someone and impress him with the consensus, and in its name deny him all hope that he could amount to anything—when we undermine his courage in this manner, and find that he does not perform, then we are not justified in saying we were right, but we must admit that *we* have caused the whole misfortune.

It is not easy in our culture for a girl to have self-confidence and courage. Incidentally, even in aptitude testing, the strange fact was shown that a certain group of girls, aged fourteen to eighteen years, were superior to all other groups, including boys. These were all girls from families in which also the woman, the mother, or she alone, had an independent occupation. This means that these girls grew up in a situation in which they did not feel the myth of the lesser capability of women, or felt it to a lesser degree, because they could see for themselves how the mother advanced through her competence. Thus these girls could develop themselves more freely and independently, almost unhampered by this myth.

EFFECTS ON WOMEN

Rebellion Against the Feminine Role[7]

The primacy of men has brought a serious disturbance into the psychological development of women, which results in women's almost general dissatisfaction with their role. They move in the same paths and under the same conditions as all

[7] A1927a, pp. 107–11.

human beings who are likely to derive from their position strong inferiority feelings. The myth of their presumed natural inferiority is an additional aggravating factor in their psychological development.

If, nevertheless, a large number of girls find a halfway satisfactory compensation, this is due to their character development, their intelligence, and perhaps certain privileges which, however, show only that one error immediately entails others. Such privileges are exemptions, luxuries, gallantries, which at least have the semblance of preference, by feigning esteem for the female. Finally, women are also idealized which, however, results in the ideal of a woman created to the advantage of the man. One woman[8] noted aptly: "The virtue of women —that is a good invention of men!"

In the struggle against the feminine role in general three types of women can be distinguished. One type will develop in an active, "masculine" direction. These women become extremely energetic, ambitious, and struggle for crowning success. They try to surpass their brothers and male comrades, turn preferably to occupations that are reserved for the male gender, engage in all sorts of sports, etc. Often they also reject love and marriage relationships. If they do enter such a relationship, they disturb it by their effort here also always to be the dominating partner, the one who is somehow superior to the other. Toward all affairs of the household they manifest an enormous aversion, either directly by frankly stating so, or indirectly by denying any talent for them—and at times also by proving that lack of talent.

This type attempts to make up for the evil by a kind of masculinity. The defensive position against the female role is a basic trait of their nature. They are sometimes called "man-women." But this is based on the erroneous conception of an innate factor, a masculine substance, that compels such girls to their attitude. However, all of cultural history shows that woman's oppression and restrictions, to which she is still subjugated, are unbearable for a person and urge her to revolt. If the revolt takes a direction that one perceives as "masculine,"

[8] George Sand (1804–76), pseudonym of the French woman novelist Amandine Dudevant.

this is due to the fact that there are after all only two possibilities to find one's way in this world—either according to the ideal manner of a woman or of a man. Thus any stepping out of the feminine role appears as masculine, and vice versa, not because of mysterious substances but because spatially and psychologically it is not possible otherwise. One must therefore keep in mind the difficulties under which a girl's development takes place. We cannot expect a complete reconciliation with life, with the facts of our culture, and the forms of our living together, as long as women are not granted equal rights with men.

Another type of woman goes through life with a kind of resignation and demonstrates an unbelievable degree of adaptation, obedience, and humility. Seemingly such women fit in anywhere, and go to work on everything, but they display such awkwardness and stupidity that they don't get anywhere, and one must become suspicious. Or they produce nervous symptoms, and emphatically present their weakness and claim for special consideration. Thereby they show how such artificial training in violation of their nature is generally punished by a nervous ailment and renders the person incapable for social life. They are the best persons in the world, but unfortunately they are ill and unable to meet the demands made on them. In the long run they are not able to satisfy their environment. Their submission, humility, and self-limitation are based on the same rebellion as in the case of the first type. They seem to say clearly: This is not a joyful life.

A third type seems to be those who, while not rejecting the feminine role, nevertheless carry within themselves the tormenting consciousness that as inferior beings they are condemned to take a subordinated role. They are fully convinced of woman's inferiority as well as the belief that only man is called upon for all the more competent performances. Thus they also advocate his privileged position. Thereby they strengthen the chorus of voices who attribute all ability only to man and demand a special position for him. They show their feeling of weakness so clearly it is as if they were seeking recognition for it and were asking for support. But this attitude also is the breaking out of the long-prepared rebellion.

It manifests itself often in a woman's marriage when she continuously turns all duties that she should fulfill herself over to her husband, admitting freely that only a man could accomplish them.

The dissatisfaction with the feminine role is even more extreme in girls who for certain "higher" reasons retreat from life by entering a convent, for example, or take up an occupation that is connected with celibacy. They belong with those who cannot be reconciled to their feminine role and in fact give up all preparations for their actual vocation. Many girls want to have a job very early to gain the independence that appears to them a protection against marrying too easily. In this attitude the disinclination toward the traditional kind of feminine role is again the driving factor.

Even when marriage is entered, where one should assume that the girl has voluntarily accepted this role, this is often no proof of reconciliation with the feminine role.

Such Women as Mothers[9]

Despite the myth of woman's inferiority, one of the most important and difficult tasks of life, the rearing of children, is left almost completely to women. This being so, what kind of parents will the three types just described make, and how will they differ?

The first type, with its masculine attitude toward life, will rule like a tyrant, will be busy with loud shouting and continuous punishment, and thus exercise strong pressure on the children, which they, of course, will try to escape. At best this will accomplish a drill that will be of no value whatever. Children usually regard such mothers as incapable of rearing them. The noise, the great uproar, and the fuss have a very bad effect, and there is the danger that the girls will be encouraged to imitate their mother, while the boys will be filled with enduring fear for the rest of their lives. Among men who were dominated by such a mother surprisingly many make a

[9] A1927a, pp. 110–11.

great detour around women, as if inoculated with bitterness, and unable to have confidence in a female. Thus a permanent discord between the sexes arises that we consider clearly pathological. Yet even in such cases there are some people who talk foolishly of a "bad distribution of masculine and feminine substance."

The other two types of women are equally unsuccessful in bringing up children. One type tends to display such a skeptical manner that the children soon notice their mother's lack of self-confidence, and get out of hand. The mother will continually renew her efforts and warnings, also threatening to tell the father. However, by always looking to the male parent, she again discloses that she has no confidence in her ability to raise her children successfully. Thus also as a parent she has her eye on retreat, as if it were up to her to justify the view that man alone is competent and therefore also indispensable in raising children. Or, such women, feeling completely incapable, refuse any educational activity and turn this responsibility over to their husband, governesses, etc.

Older Women[10]

We want to mention in this connection still another phenomenon that also frequently gives occasion for a depreciating critique of women. It is the so-called dangerous age around fifty years when certain psychological phenomena and changes along the lines of a sharpening of some character traits occur. Physical changes may suggest to a woman that she will now lose the last reminder of the slim significance she had worked so hard to maintain. Under these aggravated conditions she will increase her effort to hold onto everything that helped her before, in reaching and maintaining her position.

In our present culture, with its prevailing belief in accomplishment, older people have a difficult time altogether, but this applies even more to women. Such damage, which undermines the value of older women completely, strikes in another

[10] A1927a, pp. 116–17.

form every one of us. A calculation or evaluation of our lives cannot be made on a day-to-day basis. What one has accomplished in the full power of his years should be credited to him when he has lost his strength and effectiveness. One cannot simply exclude a person from his psychological and material connections just because he is old. The manner in which this happens to older women is practically insulting. Imagine the anxiety with which a growing girl thinks of this time, which she too will have to face one day. Being a woman is not extinguished in the fiftieth year, and human dignity also continues undiminished after this point in time, and must be preserved.

A CASE[11]

A typical example of lack of reconciliation with the feminine role is the case of a thirty-six-year-old married woman who complained about various nervous ailments. She was the older child in a marriage of an aging man and a very domineering woman. The fact that the mother, a very pretty girl, married an aging man suggests that objections against the feminine role were involved and influenced the choice of a husband. And indeed the marriage was not a good one. At home the mother shouted when she talked and enforced her will without any consideration. The old father was always pushed into the corner. The patient says that her mother often did not allow her father even to stretch out on a bench in order to rest. She was always intent on conducting her household by a principle that she had arranged by herself and that had to be considered inviolable by all.

Our patient grew up a very capable child who was much pampered by her father. Her mother, on the other hand, was never satisfied with her and was always her opponent. Later, when a boy was born, the mother greatly favored him, and her relationship with her daughter became altogether unbearable. The girl knew, however, that she had a supporter in

[11] A1927a, pp. 111–16.

her father; as indolent and compliant as he was otherwise, he could offer very vehement resistance in matters concerning his daughter.

In her stubborn struggle with her mother, the girl virtually came to hate her. A preferred object of the girl's attack was her mother's cleanliness, which went so far, for example, as not to allow a housemaid to touch a doorknob without wiping it off afterward. The girl had fun in going around as dirty and slovenly as possible and getting everything dirty. Altogether she developed only those traits that were the direct opposite of what her mother expected. This speaks very clearly against the assumption of innate characteristics. If a child develops only such traits as must vex her mother to death, this must be based on a conscious or unconscious plan. The battle continues to this day, and there is hardly a more vehement hostility.

When the patient was eight years old, approximately the following situation existed: The father was always on the side of his daughter; the mother always had a severe and angry look, and made sharp remarks and reproaches; the daughter was snappish, quick on the repartee, and countered all the efforts by her mother with unusual wit. The situation was aggravated when her younger brother, mother's favorite and likewise pampered, fell ill with a heart-valve disorder. This caused his mother's care to become even more intensive. It should be noted that the parents' efforts with regard to their children were continuously at odds. These were the circumstances under which the girl grew up.

One day she seemingly became seriously ill of a nervous ailment that no one could explain. She was constantly tormented by evil thoughts directed against her mother, which she believed hindered her in everything. Suddenly she steeped herself in religion, but without success. After a while the evil thoughts receded, which was attributed to some medication; but probably the mother was somewhat forced into a defensive position. Only a remnant of the thoughts was left, a striking fear of thunderstorms. The girl believed that the thunderstorms came only on account of her bad conscience, and that someday they would become a disaster for her on account of her evil thoughts. One sees how the child herself endeavors to free herself from the hatred against her mother.

Thus the child's development continued, and she seemed in the end yet to have a good future ahead of her. Once she was particularly impressed by one of her teachers saying, "This girl could do anything if she only wanted to." In themselves such words are insignificant. But for this girl they signified: "If she wanted to carry through something, she could do it." The result of this view was further greediness in the fight against her mother.

At the time of puberty she grew into a beautiful girl, became marriageable, and had many suitors. But through a particularly sharp tongue she again and again broke off all chances of a relationship. She felt particularly attracted only to an elderly man in the neighborhood so that one was always afraid she might marry him. But this man also went away after a while, and the girl remained without a suitor until the age of twenty-six years. This was very unusual in her circles, and no one could understand it, since they did not know her history. In the hard battle waged since childhood against her mother, she had become incompatible and quarrelsome. To fight was her victorious position. By her mother's behavior she had become irritated and led to chase constantly after triumphs. She liked nothing better than a heated argument. This showed her vanity. Her "masculine" attitude expressed itself also in her preference for games where the point was to win over an opponent.

At the age of twenty-six she met a very decent man who was not deterred by her quarrelsomeness and seriously courted her. He acted very humbly and submissively. Urged by her relatives to marry him, she declared repeatedly that she greatly disliked him and that a union with him could not end well. In view of her manner such a prophesy was not difficult. After two years' resistance she finally consented, firmly convinced to have found a slave with whom she could do what she wanted. Secretly she hoped he would be like a second edition of her father, who always gave in to her.

But soon she realized that she had been wrong. A few days after the wedding he would sit with his pipe in the living room comfortably reading his newspaper. In the morning he disappeared in his office, came punctually for dinner, and grumbled when it was not ready on time. He demanded cleanliness, affection, punctuality—in her opinion, all unjustified demands for which she was not prepared.

The relationship that developed was not at all like that between her and her father. This was a rude awakening from her dreams. The greater her demands, the less did her husband fulfill her wishes; and the more he pointed to her role of a housewife, the less he got to see of it. She continuously reminded him that he had actually no right to make such demands, since she had warned him explicitly that she did not like him. But he was not impressed. He continued to make his demands relentlessly, so that she took a very dark view of the future. This righteous, conscientious man had courted her in an intoxicated state of self-forgetting, which soon dissipated once he considered himself in secure possession.

The disharmony between them was not changed when she became a mother. She had to take on new duties. The relationship to her mother, who definitely sided with her son-in-law, became increasingly worse. Since the incessant war at home was fought with such heavy guns, the husband was at times indeed unpleasant and inconsiderate and she was in the right. Yet his behavior was a consequence of her inadequacy in and lack of reconciliation with her feminine role. If she could always have played the role of the ruler walking through life with a slave by her side who would fulfill her every wish, the marriage might perhaps have worked.

What should she do now? Should she get a divorce, or return to her mother and declare herself defeated? She could no longer become independent, as she was not prepared for this. A divorce would have violated her pride, her vanity. Life was a torment. On the one side was her husband criticizing everything; on the other, her mother with her heavy guns, always preaching cleanliness and orderliness.

Suddenly the patient became cleanly and orderly. She started scrubbing and polishing all day long. She seemed finally to have learned the lesson that her mother had always dinned into her ears. At first her mother probably smiled, and her husband was also quite pleased with the sudden orderliness of his wife, who constantly straightened out the closets.

But such a thing can also be overdone. She washed and scrubbed until everything in the house was worn. Everybody disturbed her in straightening things out, and she on her part disturbed everybody else. When she had washed something, and somebody touched it, it had to be wiped off again, and only she could do this. Yet one could rarely find as much dirt as in this woman's home, since with her it was not really a matter of cleanliness but of causing a disturbance. It fits her case that she had no girl friend, could not get along with anybody, and knew no consideration.

This so-called washing compulsion is very frequent. Such women fight against their feminine role and want in a sort of perfection to look down on the others who do not wash as often. Unconsciously these efforts aim at exploding the home.

Culture must bring us in the near future methods for the education of girls that will accomplish a better reconciliation with life. As we see this today, such reconciliation can sometimes not be attained even under the most favorable conditions. In our culture woman's inferiority, although not existent in reality and denied by all reasonable persons, is still founded in law and tradition. We must always keep this in focus, recognize the whole technique of this erroneous attitude of our social order, and fight against it not from a pathologically exaggerated veneration of the female but because such conditions are destroying our social life.

REMEDIES[12]

All these phenomena are based on errors of our culture. Once a myth has permeated a culture, it will penetrate everywhere and can be found everywhere. Thus the myth of woman's inferiority and the related overbearance of man continuously disturb the harmony of the sexes. The consequence is an enormous tension, which especially enters all love rela-

[12] A1927a, pp. 117–21.

tionships, threatening all possibilities for happiness and frequently destroying them. Our entire love life is poisoned by this tension, dries up, and becomes barren.

This is why a harmonious marriage is so rare and children grow up in the belief that marriage is something unusually difficult and dangerous. The myth about women and similar thoughts frequently prevent children from attaining a true understanding of life. Consider the many girls who regard marriage only as a kind of escape, the men and women who see in marriage only a necessary evil. The difficulties that have grown from this tension between the sexes have today taken on gigantic dimensions. They are the greater, the stronger the girl's inclination from childhood to rebel against the role forced upon her or, respectively, the greater the man's desire to play a privileged role despite the illogic that this involves.

Comradeship

The characteristic sign of conciliation, of relaxation between the sexes, is comradeship (*Kameradschaftlichkeit*). Exactly in the relationship of the sexes subordination is as unbearable as in the lives of nations. The difficulties and burdens that arise from subordination for both parties are so great that everybody should pay attention to this problem. This area is so enormous that it comprises the life of each individual. It is so complicated because our culture has charged the child with choosing his attitude toward life in a kind of opposition to the other sex.

A calm upbringing probably could master these difficulties. But the hustle of our days, the lack of really tested educational principles, and especially the competition of our entire life, have their effects as far as the nursery and give there already the directives for later life. Many persons are afraid of entering love relationships. The danger is that it has become man's task to prove his masculinity under all circumstances, even through cunning, through "conquests." This destroys the open-mindedness and confidence in love. Don Juan is undoubtedly a person who does not believe he is sufficiently manly and therefore continuously seeks new proofs for this in his conquests.

The prevailing mistrust between the sexes undermines any confidence, and thus all humanity suffers. The exaggerated ideal of masculinity represents a demand, a continuous incentive, a permanent unrest, which results in nothing but demands of vanity, self-enrichment, and privileged position, which contradict the natural conditions of humans living together.

We have no reason to oppose the present goals of the woman's movement of freedom and equal rights. Rather, we must actively support them, because ultimately happiness and joy in the life of all humanity will depend on the creation of conditions that will enable women to become reconciled with their feminine role, and on how men will answer the problem of their relationship to women.

Coeducation

Among the attempts made so far to initiate a better relationship between the sexes, coeducation is the most important. This is a controversial practice; it has its opponents and friends. The latter mention as the main advantage that it affords the sexes an opportunity to get to know one another in time, so that harmful myths can be avoided. The opponents mention primarily that the difference between boys and girls is already so great when they enter school that common education would only widen it. The boys would feel oppressed, because girls are intellectually more advanced at this time. The boys, who had to carry the entire burden of their privilege and of proof that they were more competent, would now suddenly be confronted with the realization that their privilege is only a soap bubble that dissolves in the face of reality. Some scholars also claim to have found that through coeducation boys become timid toward girls and lose their self-esteem.

Undoubtedly there is some truth to these observations and

arguments. But the arguments are only valid if one regards coeducation in the sense of a competition between the sexes, for the victory of one being more competent than the other. If understood in this way by teachers and pupils, then it is naturally harmful. Unless teachers will attain a better understanding of coeducation–one of practice of and preparation for the future co-operation of the sexes on common problems –and base their vocational activity on this conception, experiments with coeducation will always fail, and the opponents will take these failures as confirmation of their standpoint.

To give here a complete picture would require the creativity of a poet. We must be satisfied to call attention only to the main points. Coherences with the above-mentioned types are always present, and many readers will remember that the same thoughts appear here as in the description of children born with inferior organs: The growing girl often behaves as if she were inferior. In that case what was said regarding the compensation of inferiority feelings is also valid for her. The difference is that the girl receives the belief in her inferiority also from the outside. Her life is so much drawn into this path that even insightful research persons succumb at times to this myth.

The general effect of this myth is that both sexes are in the end drawn into the whirlpool of prestige politics (*Prestigepolitik*) and are playing a role with which neither part can cope. It complicates the harmlessness of their lives, robs their relationships of spontaneity, and satiates them with prejudices in the face of which any prospect of happiness disappears.[13]

CONCLUSION[14]

Perhaps the most important problem in our society is the woman question (*Frauenfrage*). Since our life is oriented toward work and earning a living, it follows that in terms of money, men demand and receive a higher price than women.

[13] A similar paragraph will be found on p. 121.
[14] Original translation from A1914f, pp. 482–83.

This situation is reflected in the minds of most people as meaning that women exist for men and their service. But this is an unnatural presupposition, based on an artificial division of the natural coherence of the sexes. Yet this myth easily originates from the occasional impediments of women, and is borne by women as well as men, usually throughout life. One may seek this evaluation not in words and conscious thoughts, but in attitudes.

From a woman's low self-esteem it follows that she easily retreats from the tests and decisions of life, having lost belief in herself. Her efforts usually weaken too soon, or by their exaltation betray a lack of confidence. The inclination toward independent action usually vanishes as early as childhood, and an excessive need to lean on something, which can rarely be satisfied, marks her achievements as inferior. The weapons of the weak, detours toward excessively high goals, and traits of submission appear, which at first seem exaggerated and soon turn into lines of domineering.

The natural meaning of the body and its organs is falsified, and all impulses are changed and poisoned by the desired and at the same time undesired goals and by the compulsion of marriage. This is because the traits of natural womanhood have been depreciated and restored only conditionally. Some highly learned authors believe to have found "innate feminine" traits in the bad sense of the word, or a feminine nature, which would condemn a person to permanent inferiority. But this is only the unfortunate outcome that we have just described, which must occur when the little girl has interiorized a masculine superstition of the hopelessness of her intellectual strivings and now continuously attempts to talk with a masculine voice. All attempts at protest, initiated to regain the belief in herself, of which she was robbed already in the nursery, only detract from the spontaneity of experiencing. When a boy meets with difficulties in his achievements, he finds help at first in the recognition of this as a general inconvenience, retains his psychological equilibrium, and can go on with his work. A girl in such cases only hears from all sides, and also from the restlessness of her own heart, "because I am only a girl"—and easily considers her effort in vain. The human soul cannot find a point of rest in such self-depreciation. The outcome is generally a hidden, but easily decoded, strange hostility toward the seemingly preferred man.

The man, for his part, burdened since childhood with the obligation to prove his superiority over women, answers the secretly hostile nature of the female sex by increased suspicion and possibly by tyranny. In view of the obvious equality of value "of all human kind" it is understandable that both sexes, from their unnatural but almost inescapable attitudes, fall heir to a permanent struggle. In consequence, they are also prone to inescapable armaments, safeguards, and skirmishes for the sake of an unnecessary prestige. Furthermore, both sexes, with very disturbing caution and increased fear, face each other as enemies, both defying each other and fearing their own defeat.

These considerations outline the severest illness of our social organism and show that these erroneous perspectives of childhood become the executors of a tragic fate. In view of this it would be wrong to point to the life lie of the refinement of our sentiments, which supposedly emerges from the battle of the sexes. To those who want to search further, I wish to point out that proofs of superiority in the relationship between men and women are almost always only pseudoproofs that advance any actual "being higher" only little. It should also be added that this appearance is often attained by forbidden devices of cunning and imagination.

APPENDIX: THE PROBLEM OF ABORTION[15]

As in most questions, so when we examine the anti-abortion law we find that only from the viewpoint of Individual Psychology can all sides of the problem be seen in proper illumination and be recognized in their true significance.

Arguments generally advanced by those who are fighting the anti-abortion law appear to the psychologist not always as

[15] Original translation of A1925i.

the most valid. I do not wish to deal here with the medical necessity on the basis of which pregnancy is often interrupted. One may assume that any physician who is not committed by a prejudice in principles, will take the position that when the life of the mother is threatened, the saving intervention must be carried out. To assess the danger correctly remains then a matter of diagnostic certainty.

Often objections against continuation of a pregnancy achieve their apparently compelling character only through the pessimistic view of the persons in question. In most of the individual cases that we examine objectively, we will find that the situation could also be regarded otherwise, more courageously, and that then the compelling reasons for an abortion would fall away.

We are often told that a family could live quite well on its income with two children, but that with a third or fourth child it would be threatened with a considerable reduction in its standard of living. But we see on the other hand often enough that it was exactly the arrival of new children that gave the parents fresh impulses toward increased activity, inspired them with new ideas for sources of income, and that instead of the feared impoverishment, a new prosperity of the whole family took place. The special difficulties in finding work and the housing shortage of our time may, naturally, in some cases aggravate this situation.

In other cases, where perhaps a young girl is endangered as an unmarried mother to lose her social position and to get into an insoluble conflict with her parents, one may frequently be able to arrive at a solution other than abortion. We have often experienced that girls who anticipated their delivery in desperation, later on saw the highest value of their life in the child and knew how to solve the difficult question of unmarried motherhood excellently. Only by this were they urged to a fruitful career that guaranteed them independence from an oppressing environment. By the same token we often see that girls who succeeded in getting rid of the undesired pregnancy, later on deplored it bitterly and realized that there would have been ways to make motherhood possible that would have brought them consolation and joy. A courageous attitude of the unmarried mother is also rather likely to encourage the partner to enter marriage. But there are also cases where we see no other way for saving the existence of the girl than by interrupting the pregnancy, especially since we cannot influence the girl's entire environment, her parents, etc.

We see then that the most important reasons given for abortion are objectively not valid. The case is usually that the pregnant woman does not want the developing child. She does not want it because in the general lack of the female sex she is afraid to fail in her life. A child, after all, means much more than the responsibility for a hungry little mouth. It means primarily a great reinforcement of the tie to the father of the child. It means surrender of the boundless egotism, of the central position, which a number of women are accustomed to take in their environment. To become pregnant and give birth also means a defeat for many women who are altogether engaged in a struggle against the superiority of the masculine sex. It means the exposure of their natural disadvantages as a woman in the area of sexuality.

But only seldom will a woman admit to herself this rejection of motherhood, because she knows that this would be an admission of egotism and cowardliness. Thus we often enough see women who are in a situation well suited for the blessing with children who are married and in good circumstances, yet are creating an artificial arrangement through which they can escape this task that is approaching them. We see women guarding their domesticity with such painstaking, "exaggerated" care, and attributing such significance to the irregularity or any interruption of the accustomed order that their entire environment automatically arrives at the thought: "How lucky that this woman has only one child!" And we shall find again and again as the root of numerous nervous disturbances, the fear of having a child.

Should one force such a woman who so strongly rejects the idea of having a child to give birth against her will? For the legislator the problem may end with the birth of the child. But we know that the problem only begins with the birth, that such a woman will by no means come to terms without protest with the undesired fact of her motherhood. What kind of a mother will she be to the child?

How can she fulfill such a difficult task when it is forced upon her against her will? One is inclined to maintain that with the birth of the child mother love will set in unconditionally, like a chemical reaction. The psychologist knows, however, that this is not always the case. Enough women let their children feel in hundreds of ways that they were unwanted when they were born. The knowledge of being an unwanted child poisons the life of many individuals, plants the root for serious psychological disturbance, and is often the basic evil from which arise delinquents and all those psychopaths who for the rest of their lives cannot get rid of the curse of a youth without love. Alone in the interest of these children—and it is primarily with regard to the children that we are judging this question—I am in favor of telling every woman plainly: "You need not have children if you don't want to."

And I have often seen that the same woman who resisted motherhood with a hundred pretenses, suddenly wanted herself the child whom she had violently rejected, once she saw herself free to decide the outcome of her pregnancy. We must never forget how deep is in each woman the protest against the inequality with men. The compulsion of a law created by men through which women are robbed of the free decision regarding their fate must be felt by every woman as a humiliation. Within this law a woman plays less the role of a person than that of a function in the interest of progeny.

Compared to this argument all others take a secondary place: Only a woman who wants the child can be a good mother to him or her.

Some parties like to maintain that the abolition of the law against abortion would worsen still further our already deplorable condition of general morals. But the low level of morality has so many other, deeper-reaching reasons—especially our entire education, which is so little oriented toward social feeling and so much toward personal ambition—that it is absurd to apply the moral lever just at this place, where one part of mankind is hit so much harder than all others. We shall well have to share the great responsibility for the ethical living together of human beings, instead of turning the heaviest burden on the weakest shoulders.

It would be a real blessing for humanity if marriage-counseling centers were created at which Individual Psychologists would function and give information on all related questions.

2

MASCULINE PROTEST AND A CRITIQUE OF FREUD

MASCULINE PROTEST[1]

Facts of Psychological Hermaphroditism

Almost every investigator of human hermaphroditism has mentioned or emphasized that among the derived sexual characteristics one often finds psychological traits of the other sex. Krafft-Ebing, Dessoir, Halban, Fliess, Freud, and Hirschfield are among these.

Freud has studied particularly the phenomena of homosexuality in neurosis and found that every neurotic shows homosexual traits. This observation has been amply confirmed. [*Later replaced by:* I have been able to correct this observation as a frequent sign of the irreconcilability of neurosis with eroticism.] In a small paper (A1908f) I have pointed out the relationship of prostitution to homosexuality. Fliess believed earlier that the male neurotic suffered from suppression of his feminine traits; the female neurotic, from repression of her masculine traits. Sadger held similar ideas.

A careful study of the neuroses with regard to traits of hermaphroditism yields the following results:

[1] Translation of A1910c, "Psychological Hermaphroditism in Life and Neurosis: On the Dynamics and Therapy of Neuroses," as reprinted in A1914a, pp. 74–83; 1928 ed., pp. 76–84.

1. General physical phenomena of the opposite sex are found remarkably often—feminine habitus in male neurotics, and masculine habitus in female neurotics. Secondary characteristics of the opposite sex are likewise often found: in men—inferiority phenomena of the genitals, such as hypospadias [congenital opening of the urethra on the underside of the penis], para-urethral passages, small penis, small testicles, cryptorchidism [concealment of one or both testes within the abdomen], etc., and in women—large labium minus, large clitoris, infantilism of the sexual apparatus, etc. Additionally, we find as a rule inferiorities of other organs. (See A1907a.)

Whether these physical phenomena bear right from the start any genetic relationship to the opposite-sex psyche, as Fliess assumes and as Krafft-Ebing specified, so that in the man the feminine psyche, in the woman the masculine psyche would be more strongly developed, cannot be proven at present [*later added:* with certainty].

It can be shown, however, in children with inferior organs, organ systems, and glandular systems, that their mobility and physical development often deviate from the norm, that their growth and functioning show deficiencies, and that sickness and weakness are prominent, especially at the beginning of their development, although these may later on often give way to robust health and strength.

2. These objective phenomena frequently give rise to a subjective feeling of inferiority and thus hinder the independence of the child, increase his need for support and affection, and characterize the adult person, often until old age. Weakness, clumsiness, awkwardness, sickliness, childhood disorders such as enuresis, incontinence of the feces, stuttering, shortage of breath, deficiencies in the visual and auditory apparatus, innate or early acquired blemishes, and extreme ugliness, etc., may all give a deep foundation for the feeling of inferiority in relation to stronger persons and fixate it for life. This is especially true of the feeling toward the father. Significant traits of obedience, submission, and devoted love toward the father

characterize many children, especially those disposed toward neurosis.[2]

Such children are thus often placed in a role that appears to them as unmanly. All male neurotics as children were moved by doubt regarding their achievement of full masculinity. The renunciation of masculinity, however, appears to the child as synonymous with femininity. Thereby a wide area of originally childish value judgments is given: Any uninhibited aggression, activity, competence, power, and the traits of being brave, free, rich, aggressive, or sadistic can be considered as masculine; all inhibitions and deficiencies, as well as cowardliness, obedience, poverty, and similar traits, as feminine (see A1908b).[3]

3. The child plays a double role for a while. On the one hand, he shows tendencies of submission to the parents and educators, and on the other hand, some of his wishes, fantasies, and actions express a striving for independence, a will of his own, and significance ("the little would-be-great"). Since girls and women display more of the one tendency, and boys and men more of the other, the child arrives at value judgments similar to those of the adults: to regard inhibition of aggression as feminine, increased aggression itself as masculine. "To be bad" often means for the child to be masculine.

This inner disunion in the child is the example and foundation of the most important psychological phenomena especially of the neurosis, the [*later added:* falsely so-called] splitting of consciousness and [*later added:* starting point of] indecision, and may result in various outcomes in later life. As a rule one will find attitudes of an individual varying between the "feminine" and the "masculine" directions, together with tendencies to strengthen the unity of the picture from within. After all, males are impeded from complete merging into the feminine role, and vice versa. This leads usually to a compromise—that is [in men], feminine deport-

[2] See also C. G. Jung (1909). [Author's note, omitted from later editions.]

[3] Incidentally, this evaluation holds not only for the child, but also for the greater part of our cultural consciousness. [Author's note.]

ment with masculine means (for example, masculine shyness and submission, masculine masochism, homosexuality, etc.), and [in women] masculine role with feminine means (emancipation tendencies of women, polyandry, compulsion neurosis as disturbance of the feminine role, etc.). Or one finds an apparently haphazard side-by-side of "masculine" and "feminine" traits.

In neurosis, where we are always dealing with the incongruencies of such traits, their discernment and reduction are possible with the methods of Individual Psychology. The precondition, however, is that the therapist does not bring his own value judgments about masculine and feminine traits to the analysis but adapts himself to the feelings of the patient and follows these.

The Masculine Protest[4]

The starting point for the feminine tendencies of the neurotic is the child's feeling of weakness in the face of adults. From this arises a need for support, a demand for affection, a physiological and psychological dependency and submission. In cases of early and subjectively felt organ inferiority (motor weakness, clumsiness, sickliness, childhood disorder, slow development, etc.), these traits are intensified, whereby the dependency grows. This increased feeling of one's own smallness and weakness (the root of the delusion of smallness) leads to inhibition of aggression and thereby to anxiety. The uncertainty regarding one's competence releases doubts, a vacillation between the "feminine" tendencies (anxiety and related phenomena) and the "masculine" tendencies (aggression, compulsion phenomena). The structure of the neuroses (neurasthenia, hysteria, phobia, paranoia, and especially compulsion neurosis) shows the often ramified "feminine" lines carefully hidden and covered over by hypertrophied "masculine" wishes and tendencies.

[4] See Schiller, "The Dignity of Men": "I am a man. . . ." [Author's note.]

This is the masculine protest. It follows necessarily as overcompensation when the "feminine" tendency is valued negatively by the childish judgment, somewhat like a childhood disorder, and is retained only in sublimated form and on account of external advantages (love of one's relatives, freedom from punishment, praise for obedience, subordination, etc.).

Every form of inner compulsion in normal, and neurotic individuals may be derived from this attempt at a masculine protest. Where it succeeds, it naturally strengthens the masculine tendencies enormously; posits for itself the highest and often unattainable goals; develops a craving for satisfaction and triumph; intensifies all abilities and egotistical drives; increases envy, avarice, and ambition; and brings about an inner restlessness that makes any external compulsion, lack of satisfaction, disparagement, and injury unbearable. Defiance, vengeance, and resentment are its steady accompaniments. Through a boundless increase in sensitivity, it leads to continuous conflicts. Normal and pathological fantasies of grandeur and daydreams are forced by such overly strong masculine protest and are experienced as provisional surrogates of drive satisfaction. Dream life also comes entirely under the dominance of the masculine protest. Every dream, when analyzed, shows the tendency to move away from the feminine line toward the masculine line.

The masculine protest is equally valid for women as for men, only that in women it is usually covered and changed, and seeks to triumph with feminine means. Very often one finds during the analysis the wish to change into a man. Vaginism, sexual anesthesia [frigidity], and many well-known neurotic phenomena originate from this tendency.

If one follows the "dynamic approach" that I have suggested, one will soon recognize that all these phenomena have in common the striving somehow to gain distance from the feminine line and to gain the masculine line. Thus neurotic symptoms are sometimes more feminine, sometimes more masculine, and every neurotic symptom represents a hermaphrodite.

The neurotic compulsion shows the masculine protest; to

succumb to the compulsion is feminine–for example, in compulsive blushing (erythrophobia), the patient reacts with (masculine) rage and temper to felt or feared depreciation. But the reaction takes place with feminine means, with blushing or fear of blushing. The meaning of the attack is: "I am a woman and want to be a man."

Thus the neurotic safeguards himself from decisions that appear dangerous–for example, by substituting a compulsion of his own for one from without (Furtmüller, 1912).

If the patient finds himself cut off from all personal success, if the satisfaction of his usually overreaching masculine protest has failed in a main line, in which the sex drive, though always included, is only one of the components, then the neurosis, toward which steps have long since been taken, finally breaks out. The patient then tries to satisfy his masculine ambition on side lines through displacement onto other persons and goals; or, the inhibition and blocking become more intensive, and such transformations of the aggression drive result as I have described in my paper entitled "The Aggression Drive in Life and Neurosis" (A1908b).[5]

The aggression drive and its transformations play the most important role in neurosis. [But] this conception suffered from the defect of being biological and not suitable to a complete understanding of neurotic phenomena. To this end, one must consider a conception of the neurotic that is most highly personal and judges phenomena in a way that does not admit of definitions in biological terms, but only in psychological terms, or in terms of cultural psychology.

It is my proposition, then–consonant with that of Freud–that in every neurotic (in every human being) we find masculine as well as feminine traits, whether it be in mixed (compromise) formation, or one alongside the other. The sublimated form of this conception is the problem of freedom

[5] Aggression drive is used by Adler not exclusively in the sense of hostility, as is generally done today, but also in the sense of an active assertion. George A. Kelly (1963, p. 143) has since then made the similar distinction between hostility and aggression, where aggression is a dimensional trait, with inertia and initiative as the two poles.

or the determination of the will. Despite our inner conviction that the will is determined, we behave as if it were free; the fault lies in the posing of the problem. In a similar way, these two distinct conceptions are felt by the neurotic, and all character traits can be traced back to that fact.[6]

The Structure of Neurosis

For the structure of the neurosis all these variations gain great significance. The feminine, masochistic tendency (in the opinion of the patient) predominates and creates the feminine, masochistic picture of the neurosis, while at the same time the patient becomes endowed with extreme sensitivity against any sinking into "femininity," against any depreciation, oppression, curtailment, and defilement.

The weak point, the feeling of inferiority, the feminine lines are covered up or are masked by compromise formation, or are made unrecognizable through sublimation and symbolization. But they gain in breadth and intensity, continuously or occasionally, and become manifest in the form of abulia, ill humor, depression, anxiety, pain, feeling of anxious expectation, doubt, paralysis, impotence, insufficiency, etc.

The feeling of inferiority thus whips up the drive life, increases the wishes boundlessly, provokes oversensitivity, and creates a craving for satisfaction that tolerates no adaptation and results in continuous, overheated expectations and fears. In this hypertrophied craving, passion for success, frantic masculine protest, lies the germ of failure—but also the predestination for the achievements of the genius and the artist.

The neurosis breaks out when the masculine protest has failed in a main line. The feminine traits then apparently predominate, but only under continuous increase of the masculine protest and pathological attempts to break through along masculine side lines. Such attempts may succeed without bringing real satisfaction and harmony, or they may fail,

[6] This and the preceding paragraph reprinted from A1910n, p. 425 and pp. 425–26, respectively.

as often in neurosis, and force the patient further into the feminine role, apathy, anxiety, and mental, physical, and sexual insufficiency, etc., which are further exploited as means for power.

The investigation of full-fledged neurosis, in view of the above, will always reveal the following traits and note their dynamic valences:

a. feminine traits [*later:* traits evaluated as feminine].
b. hypertrophied masculine protest.
c. compromise formation between a and b.

The failure of the masculine protest in the case of psychological hermaphroditism is favored, practically brought about, through the following factors:

1. Exaggeration of the protest. The goal is as such, or with regard to the patient's resources, unattainable.

2. Overestimation of the goal. Such overestimation (as by Don Quixote) is unconsciously purposeful, so as not to disturb the hero role of the patient. In this way disappointments are bound to result.

3. Feminine tendencies setting the tone and inhibiting aggression. Often at the crucial moment or before the intended action, the "feminine" feeling awakens in the form of exaggerated belief in authority, doubt, and anxiety, and leads to humiliation and submission under continuous protest formation, or it forges a weapon from doubt, anxiety, etc., and thus leads the submission to absurdity.

4. An active guilt feeling (see A1909a) [*later added:* a descendant of social interest] that is derived from childhood and [whose objects] can easily be shifted. It supports the feminine traits and frightens the patient with possible consequences of his deed (the Hamlet type).

Reinforcement of Feminine Lines

At this point I must mention further reinforcers of the feminine lines in the child that go more or less beyond the physiological measure and regularly represent the occasions for exaggerating the masculine protest. I was able to recognize the following origins and mechanisms in a considerable number of neurotics of both sexes, so that I may well speak of a general validity of these findings, all the more so since by their uncovering, the cure of the neurosis was initiated.

1. Fear of punishment. It is furthered by overreacting to pain and oversensitivity of the skin, strictness of the educators, and corporal punishment. To be taken as masculine reactions are: indifference toward punishment, defiant indifference, the bearing of pain, often seeking of tortures (apparent masochism, see Wexberg, 1914), and the patient's demonstrative assertions of how much he can stand, erection and active sexual behavior when threatened with punishment, which may sometimes be facilitated by individual physiological peculiarities (see Asnaourow, 1913).

2. Seeking sympathy by demonstrating one's weakness or suffering. Or, masculine protest: ideas of grandeur (in compensation for the feminine delusion of smallness), indignation about the sympathy of others, laughing instead of crying [*later added:* cynicism, fight against stirrings of affection], etc., making fun of oneself. Combinations occur regularly. Childhood disorders such as enuresis, stuttering, sickliness, headaches, lack of appetite, etc., may become fixated through counting on sympathy or out of defiance. Almost regularly, compromise formations occur. The masculine reaction uses weakness to annoy the parents and is defiant by retaining a disorder so as not to have to give in. All [*later:* Many] enuretic dreams show the attempt of the dreamer to act like a man (to urinate standing up, urinal for men, large arc of the urine stream, urinating figures in the sand). At the same time this is a masculine reaction against fear of punishment, often with use of fictions, as if the chamber pot or the toilet were available.

3. Erroneous conception of the sexual roles, ignorance of the difference between man and woman, and thoughts about the possibility of a transformation of boys into girls and vice versa. Frequently there is a dim feeling of being a her-

maphrodite. Physical attributes, errors in upbringing, misunderstood utterances from the environment (girls' clothing on boys, long hair on boys, short hair on girls, bathing together with the other sex, dissatisfaction of the parents with the sex of the child, etc.) awaken or increase the child's doubt as long as the sex differences are not clear to him. Similarly, fairy tales regarding the birth of children or false conceptions of it (birth through the anus; conception through the mouth, through a kiss, through poison, or through touching) create confusion. Deviating early sexual experiences or fantasies in which the mouth or the anus plays the role of the sex organ contribute to blurring the distinction between man and woman and may become fixated in a biased way.

Sexual Disorders

Homosexuality originates from the attempt to change the sexual role [*later:* from the uncertainty of one's sexual role]. Homosexual men had in childhood the talent to think themselves into a girl's role. If, as always, the masculine protest occurs, the transformation into a homosexual takes place as avoidance of the feared woman.

Altogether, understanding can be attained only if one follows the masculine attempts at protest, as for example in compulsory masturbation which, like any compulsion, means the attempt to do like a man and yet evade one's sexual role [*later:* one's task]. The same tendency is found in pollution and ejaculatio praecox. The haste as well as the accompanying phenomena (insufficient erection, sometimes homosexual dreams) betray the weak point hidden behind these. In the analysis of dreams one should look for nightmares, dreams of being prevented from something, and dreams of anxiety that belong to an elaboration of the feminine line, a defeat. Yet in these dreams almost regularly the masculine tendency breaks through (screaming, fleeing, awakening)—as protest.

Exhibitionistic traits are favored by the tendency to show oneself as a man [*later added:* despite the feeling of insecurity]. In girls and women a renunciation of female modesty or the rejection of female garments seems to be sufficient for this purpose. The same tendency for power characterizes narcissism. In fetishism the unmanly line regularly becomes prevalent (preference for lingerie, blouses, aprons, jewelry, hairpieces, etc. [*later added:* instead of the partner]), but is always accompanied by the masculine tendency not to be dominated by the partner. Originally an expression of hermaphroditism like every autoeroticism, [glove and] shoe fetishism [are] directed toward the cover [*later:* the incidental thing] and [gain their] feminine, masochistic character through their distance from the masculine role. [*Later added:* The evasion from an assumed danger zone always becomes apparent.]

Originally masochistic traits, like hypochondriases and exaggerated sensitivity to pain, belong with the "feminine" traits of endurance. Like any psychological phenomenon, they never lack further incidental determiners to demonstrate the size of the suffering, etc. [*later added:* and to withdraw from fulfilling the life tasks in presentiment of a defeat].

It is very understandable that the child uses the traits of his mother to represent his feminine lines, and those of his father for his masculine lines. ("From father I have the stature. . . .") The masculine protest intensifies the desires of the child, who then seeks to surpass his father in every respect and comes into conflicts with him. Thus those secondary traits arise that correspond to desires aimed at the mother (Oedipus allegory).

Therapy

It is the task of education and psychotherapy to uncover this dynamic and make it conscious. Thereby the biased overgrowth of the "feminine and masculine traits" will disappear, and the childish valuation give room to a more mature world view; likewise, the dissociative processes, split consciousness, and *double vie* will stop. The oversensitivity gives way, and the patient learns to tolerate the tensions from the environment without becoming upset. Whereas he was before "a toy of dark unconscious stirrings, he becomes the conscious master or sufferer of his feelings" (A1905b) [reference later omitted].[7]

ANTITHETICAL APPERCEPTION AND DOGMATIZATION[8]

We consider the guiding force of the neurosis to be the desire for the enhancement of the self-esteem as the final purpose. This force always tries to assert itself with special strength. It is the expression of a striving and wanting, which is deeply rooted in human nature. This guiding thought could also be called "will to power" (Nietzsche). Its expression and deepening informs us that a particular compensatory force is involved to put an end to the general human insecurity.

By a rigid formulation, which usually rises to the surface of consciousness, the neurotic tries to gain a firm basis to unhinge the world. It does not really matter whether he is conscious of much or little of this driving force. In either case he neither knows the mechanism nor is he able by himself to uncover and break up his childish analogical behavior and apperception. This succeeds only with the method of Individual Psychology, which permits one to guess and to understand the childish analogy by means of abstraction, reduction, and simplification, and by the observation of the nearly content-free psychological movement.

It turns out that the neurotic apperceives always according to the analogy of an antithesis and usually even knows and admits only antithetical relationships. This primitive orientation in the world, which corresponds to the antithetical categories of Aristotle, as well as to the Pythagorean tables of opposites, originates in the feeling of insecurity and represents a

[7] The original reference actually reads: "The helpless toys of bad moods and depressions will become conscious opponents or sufferers of an imposed destiny."

[8] Translated from A1912a, 1928 ed. Most of these selections have appeared also in A1956b, pp. 246–50.

simple device of logic. What I have described as polar hermaphroditic opposites (A1910c), Lombroso[9] as bipolar, and Bleuler[10] as ambivalent, leads back to this mode of apperception, which functions according to the principle of antithesis.

One must not fall into the common error of regarding this as an essence of things, but must recognize in it the primitive working method, a point of view, which measures a thing, a force, or an experience by an opposite that is fitted to it.

Antithetical Apperception

The neurotically disposed individual has a sharply schematizing, strongly abstracting mode of apperception. Thus he groups inner as well as outer events according to a strictly antithetical schema, something like the debit and credit sides in bookkeeping, and admits no degrees in between. This mistake in neurotic thinking, which is identical with exaggerated abstraction, is also caused by the neurotic safeguarding tendency. This tendency needs sharply defined guiding lines, ideals, and bogeys in which the neurotic believes, in order to choose, foresee, and take action.

In this way he becomes estranged from concrete reality, where psychological elasticity is needed rather than rigidity—that is, where the use of abstraction is needed rather than its worship and deification. After all, there is no principle to live by that would be valid to the very end; even the most correct solutions of problems interfere with the course of life when they are pushed too far into the foreground, as, for example, if one makes cleanliness and truth the goal of all striving.

In the psychological life of the neurotic we find the inclination to stylize experiences and persons in the environment to a very pronounced degree, exactly as we find it in primitive thought, mythology, legend, cosmogeny, theogeny, primitive art, psychotic productions, and the beginnings of philosophy. In this process phenomena that do not belong together must,

[9] Cesare Lombroso (1836–1909), Italian psychiatrist.
[10] Eugen Bleuler (1857–1939), Swiss psychiatrist.

of course, be sharply separated by abstractive fiction. The urge to do this comes from the desire for orientation which, in turn, originates in the safeguarding tendency. This urge is often so considerable that it demands artificial dissection of the unity, the category, and even the self into two or several antithetical parts.

One of the pairs of opposites often becomes increasingly clear: inferiority feeling vs. enhancement of self-esteem. To resort to concrete pairs of opposites corresponds to the primitive attempts of the child to orient himself in the world and to safeguard himself. Among these pairs I have regularly found: (1) *above-below* and (2) *masculine-feminine.* In the sense of the patient, but not always in the general sense, memories, impulses, and actions are then always arranged by a classification of *inferior = below = feminine* vs. *powerful = above = masculine.* This classification is important. Because it can be falsified and advanced at will, it affords a distortion of the picture of the world by which the neurotic can always retain his standpoint of having been humiliated. It lies in the nature of things that here the patient's experiences of his constitutional inferiority come to his assistance, as does the increasing aggression of his environment, which is continuously irritated by his neurotic behavior.

The neurotic's striving for security, his very safeguards, can be understood when the original antithetic value-factor, namely that of insecurity, is taken into consideration. Both security and insecurity are the result of a dichotomizing judgment that has become dependent upon the fictional personality ideal and furnishes biased subjective value judgments. The feeling of security and its opposite pole, the feeling of insecurity, arranged according to the antithesis of inferiority feeling and personality ideal, are, like the latter, a fictional pair of values. They are the kind of psychological construction concerning which Vaihinger (1911) points out "that in them reality is artificially divided, that they have meaning and value only when together, but that, when taken singly, they lead through their isolation to meaninglessness, contradictions, and illusionary problems."

In the analysis of psychoneuroses it often becomes apparent that these antitheses are analogous to the antithesis of man–woman taken for real. The dynamics of the neurosis can therefore be regarded, and are often so understood by the neurotic, "as if" the patient wished to change from a woman to a man or wanted to hide his unmanliness. These tendencies, in their varied fullness, give the picture of what I have called the *masculine protest*.

Dogmatized Guiding Fiction

The neurotic carries his feeling of insecurity constantly with him. Therefore, "analogical thinking"—that is, the attempted solution of problems according to the analogy of former experiences—is more strongly and distinctly expressed in him than in normal individuals. His fear of the new (the *misoneism* of Lombroso) and of decisions and tests, which always confront one, originates from his deficient self-confidence. He has chained himself so much to guiding lines, takes them so literally, and seeks to realize them so much, to the exclusion of any alternative, that unknowingly he has renounced the unprejudiced, open-minded approach to questions of reality.

The feeling of insecurity forces the neurotic to a stronger attachment to fictions, guiding lines, ideals, and principles. These guiding principles are envisaged by the normal person also. But to him they are a figure of speech (*modus dicendi*), a device for distinguishing above from below, left from right, right from wrong; he does not lack the open-mindedness, when called upon to make a decision, to free himself from these fictions, and to reckon with reality. Neither are the world's phenomena for him divided into rigid antitheses; on the contrary, he strives constantly to keep his thoughts and actions detached from the unreal guiding line and to bring them into harmony with reality. The fact that he uses fictions at all as a means to an end arises from the usefulness of the fiction in casting up the accounts of life.

The neurotic, however, like the dependent child still removed from the world, and like primitive man, clings to the straw of his fiction, hypostasizes it—that is, arbitrarily ascribes reality to it, and seeks to realize it in the world. For this the fiction is unfit; it is still more unfit when, as in the psychoses, it is elevated to a dogma or anthropomorphized. "Act 'as if' you were lost, 'as if' you were the biggest, 'as if' you were the most hated." The symbol as a *modus dicendi* dominates our speech and thought. The neurotic takes it literally, and the psychotic attempts its realization. In my contributions to the theory of the neuroses this point is always emphasized and maintained.

More firmly than the normal individual does the neurotic fixate his god, his idol, his personality ideal, and cling to his guiding line, and with deeper purpose he loses sight of reality. The normal person, on the other hand, is always ready to dispense with this aid, this crutch. In this instance, the neurotic resembles a person who looks up to God, commends himself to the Lord, and then waits credulously for His guidance; the neurotic is nailed to the cross of his fiction. The normal individual, too, can and will create his deity, will feel drawn upward. But he will never lose sight of reality, and always take it into account as soon as action and work are demanded. The neurotic is under the hypnotic spell of a fictional life plan.

I readily follow here the ingenious views of Vaihinger, who maintains that historically ideas tend to grow from fictions (unreal but practically useful constructs) to hypotheses and later to dogmas. In Individual Psychology this change of intensity differentiates in a general way the thinking of the normal individual (fiction as an expedient), of the neurotic (attempt to realize the fiction), and of the psychotic (incomplete but safeguarding anthropomorphism and reification of the fiction: dogmatization).

An example of this progression would be the intensification of cautiousness into anxiety, and occasionally the reification of the anticipation of disaster into depression. These three steps of achieving security may be clarified as follows. Caution (normal, fiction): "as if" I could lose my money, "as if" I could be below. Anxiety (neurotic, hypothesis): "as if" I were *going* to lose my money, "as if" I were *going* to be below. Depression (psychotic, dogma): "as if" I *had* lost my money, "as if" I were below. In other words, the stronger the feeling of insecurity, the more accentuated the fiction becomes through increasing abstraction from reality, and the more it approaches dogma. The patient nourishes and feigns within himself everything that brings him nearer to his guiding line, which in turn gives him security and thus is effective, albeit in a reduced circle. In this process reality becomes devaluated in various degrees, and the corrective paths that are adapted to society prove themselves increasingly insufficient.

CRITIQUE OF FREUD'S LIBIDO THEORY[11]

Less to be critical than to bring out my own viewpoint, may I separate from the fruitful and valuable contributions of Freud especially three of his fundamental views as erroneous, since they threaten to block progress in the understanding of neurosis.

Libido, Subject to Purpose, "Will to Power"

The first objection concerns the understanding of libido as the driving force in neurosis. Exactly neurosis, more clearly than normality, shows that a purpose forces the feeling of pleasure, its modification and its strength, into its own direction. Thus the neurotic can, so to speak, only with the healthy part of his psychological energy follow the allurement of attaining pleasure, whereas for the neurotic part "higher" goals are in operation. [*Later added:* If "libido" is translated into "love" with its many meanings, then by a clever use and expansion of these any event in the cosmos can be paraphrased by it—but not explained. By this paraphrasing many people get the impression that any human impulse is full of "libido," whereas in reality the lucky finder only extracts what he first put into it. Freud's latest interpretations seem as if his libido

[11] Translated from A1912a, 1928 ed., pp. 2–5.

theory moved rapidly toward our standpoint of social interest and the striving toward a personality ideal ("ego ideal"). In the interest of a growing understanding, this is to be greatly welcomed.]

We have found the neurotic purpose to be the enhancement of the self-esteem [*Erhöhung des Persönlichkeitsgefühls*], the simplest formula of which can be recognized in the exaggerated masculine protest. This formula, "I want to be a real man," is the guiding fiction [*later added:* so to speak the fundamental apperception (Jerusalem)[12]] in every neurosis, for which it claims greater reality value than the normal psyche. To this guiding idea are subordinated the libido, the sex drive, and any inclination to deviation, whatever their origin. Nietzsche's "will to power" and "will to seem" include much of our conception, which also touches in many points on the views of Féré[13] and older authors, according to whom the feeling of pleasure is rooted in the feeling of power, that of displeasure in the feeling of powerlessness.[14]

Sexual Etiology, a Metaphor

A second objection concerns Freud's basic view of the sexual etiology of the neurosis. Previously Pierre Janet (1894) had come precariously close to this view when he raised the question, "Should, then, the sexual feeling be the center, around which the other psychological syntheses are constructed?" The usefulness of the sexual metaphor leads many, especially the neurotic, to believe it to be an identity. [*Later added:* We frequently find among mystics—for example, Baader[15]—such expressions. Language also, with its incli-

[12] Wilhelm Jerusalem (1854–1923), Austrian educator, philosopher, close to pragmatism, translator of William James' *Pragmatism*.
[13] Charles S. Féré (1852–1907), French physician, student of Charcot.
[14] Eventually Adler replaced "will to power" with "striving toward overcoming."
[15] Franz Xavier von Baader (1765–1841), German mystic and professor of philosophy in Munich.

nation toward analogy, sets considerable traps for the unsuspecting investigator.] This usefulness must not deceive the psychologist.

The sexual content in the neurosis originates primarily in the conceived antithesis of "masculine-feminine" and is a change in form from the masculine protest. The sexual impetus in the fantasy and the life of the neurotic is oriented toward the masculine purpose; it is really no drive at all, but a compulsion. The entire syndrome of the sexual neurosis is a metaphor that reflects the patient's distance from his fictitious masculine final goal, and his attempts to overcome or perpetuate it.

It is strange that Freud, a connoisseur of the symbolic in life, was incapable of resolving the symbolic in the sexual apperception, to recognize the sexual as a jargon, as a *modus dicendi.*

Infantile Wishes Compelled by Goal

But we can understand this when we regard the third basic mistake, Freud's assumption that the neurotic is under the compulsion of infantile wishes [*later added:* especially the incest wish]. These wishes were assumed to come to life every night (dream theory), but also on certain occasions in reality. But in reality all infantile wishes themselves are already under the compulsion of the fictive final goal, have usually themselves the character of a guiding but co-ordinated thought, and for reasons of economy of thought are very well suited as symbols for calculating.

A sick girl who, feeling particularly insecure, leans on her father during her entire childhood, and thereby wants to be superior to her mother, can occasionally formulate this psychological constellation as the "incest parable," as if she wanted to be her father's wife. But thereby her final purpose is already given and effective: to have her insecurity contained by being with her father. Her growing psychomotor intelligence, her unconsciously affected memory answer all feelings of insecurity with the same aggression: with the preparatory attitude to seek refuge with her father as if she were his wife. There she finds the higher self-esteem that she has posited as her purpose and that she borrowed from the masculine ideal of her childhood, the overcompensation of her inferiority feeling.

When she is frightened by a courtship or marriage, insofar as these threaten new depreciations of her self-esteem [*later added:* insofar as she finds greater difficulties than with her father], she acts symbolically. Her readiness is purposefully turned against a feminine destiny, and lets her seek security where she has always found it—with her father. She applies a device, acts according to a nonsensical fiction, but thereby can certainly attain her purpose [*later added:* to avoid the feminine role].

The greater her feeling of insecurity, the more does this girl cling to her fiction and try to take it almost literally. Since human thinking is inclined toward symbolic abstraction, the patient sometimes—and with some effort, the analyst also—succeeds in capturing the neurotic striving for security in the symbol of an incest impulse [*later added:* to be superior as with her father].

In this purposeful process Freud had to see a revival of infantile wishes because he had assumed the latter as driving forces. We recognize in this infantile working method, in the extensive application of safeguarding working hypotheses as which we must regard the neurotic fiction, in this total longstanding preparation, in this tendency toward strong abstraction and symbolization, the appropriate means of the neurotic who wants to reach security, enhancement of his self-esteem, the masculine protest.

[*Later added:* The neurosis shows us the execution of erroneous intentions. All thinking and acting can be traced back to childhood experiences. Thus, regarding Freud's "regression," the psychologically ill person does not differ from one who is well. The difference is only that the psychologically ill person builds upon errors that go too far, and that he takes a poor attitude toward life. In itself, regression is the normal form of thinking and acting.]

SEXUALITY IN NEUROSIS[16]

Limited Role of Sexuality

The sex drive is of similar importance in everybody's life. Thus it would be an idle question to ask if a neurosis is possible without it. The question rather is, whether the sex drive is to be regarded as the beginning and end of everything, including the formation of all neurotic symptoms. To this I wish to reply with a brief description, not of the isolated sex drive, but of its development in the ensemble of all drives.

Biologically speaking, it would not be possible to maintain that every drive has a sexual component, including the drive to eat, the drive to see, and the drive to touch, etc. One must assume rather that organic evolution has led to developments that we must regard as the differentiation of originally present potentialities of the cell. Thus a nutritive organ has followed the will and need of assimilation; touch, auditory, and visual organs have followed the will and necessity to feel, hear, and see; a procreative organ followed the will and necessity for progeny.

The protection of all these organs became so necessary that it was approached from two sides: through the sensation of pain and that of pleasure. But these were not enough, and thus a third safeguard developed in the form of the organ of prudence, the organ of thinking, the brain. In the laboratory of nature, variations of all three safeguards can be found. Peripheral defects as well as heightened sensations of pain and pleasure in an inferior organ may occur. The most variable part, the central nervous system, takes over the final compensation.

The statement that the child is a polymorphous pervert, is a *hysteron proteron* [reverses the order of things], is a poetic license. The "sexual constitution" can be cultivated at will

16 Translated with some omissions from A1911a as published in A1914a, 1928 ed., pp. 92–95. Parts of this translation have appeared in A1956b, pp. 56–60.

through experiences and education, especially on the basis of organ inferiorities. Even prematurity can be kept down or advanced. Sadistic and masochistic impulses are simply developments from the more harmless relationships of the regularly present need for support and the impulse toward independence once the masculine protest is involved with its intensification of rage, anger, and defiance.

Only the sexual organ, and it alone, develops the sexual factor in life in general and in the neurosis. As sexuality enters relations with the total drive life and its causes, so does every other drive. Approximately at the end of the first year of life—before the sex drive reaches a notable degree—the psychological life of the child is already richly developed.

Defiance, and Valuation of Masculinity

Freud mentions the view of older authors, who were later joined by Czerny,[17] that children who are stubborn on the toilet often become nervous. In contrast to other authors, Freud traces this defiance to their having sexual pleasure feelings during retention of feces. Although I have seen no incontestable case of this sort, I agree that children who do have such sensations when they retain feces will prefer precisely this kind of resistance when they become defiant. The decisive factor is the defiance, while the inferior organ determines the localization and selection of the symptoms.

I have much more frequently observed that such defiant children produce the feces before or after they have been brought to the toilet, or right next to the toilet; the same is true of the urination of such children. It is the same with eating and drinking; we need only to curb the drinking of certain children, and their "libido" increases into infinity. We need only to tell them that eating regularly is important, and their libido drops to zero. Can we take such "libido quantities" seriously, let alone energetically, and use them for comparisons? I have seen a thirteen-month-old boy who had

[17] Adalbert Czerny (1863–1941), German pediatrician.

barely learned to stand and to walk. If we sat him down, he got up; if we told him, "Sit down," he remained standing and looked mischievous. His six-year-old sister said on one such occasion, "Keep standing," and the child sat down. These are the beginnings of the masculine protest. The sexuality that is meanwhile budding is continuously exposed to its impacts and urges.

The valuation of masculinity also begins remarkably early. I have seen one-year-old boys and girls who evidently preferred male persons. Perhaps it is the sound of the voice, the assured appearance, the size, the strength, the calm that make the difference. I have pointed to this valuation critically in a review (A1910m) of Jung's "On Conflicts of the Soul of the Child," and as I see presently, with some success (see Hitschmann, and Jung, 1913). It regularly gives rise to the wish to become a man.

The other day I heard a little boy of two years say: "Mamma dumb, Nanny dumb, Toni [the cook] dumb, Usi [the sister] dumb, Gramma dumb!" When asked if Grampa was also dumb, he said: "Grampa big." Everybody noted that he had excepted his father. This was taken as a sign of respect. But one could easily understand that he wanted to declare all female members of his surroundings as stupid, himself and the male members as intelligent. He identified stupid with feminine, intelligent with masculine. This equation gave him importance.

I have pointed out in several papers that especially children who have a noticeable organ inferiority, who suffer from defects, who are insecure, and who fear humiliation and punishment the most, develop the craving and haste that ultimately dispose to neurosis. At an early age they will avoid tests of their worth or evade injuries to their sensitivity. They are bashful, blush easily, evade any test of their ability, and lose at an early age their spontaneity. This uncomfortable condition strongly urges toward safeguards. They want to be petted or want to do everything alone, are afraid of any kind of work, or read incessantly. As a rule they are precocious. Their thirst for knowledge is a compensatory product of their insecurity and reaches at an early age toward questions about birth and sex differences. This strained and continuous fantasy activity must be understood as a stimulus for the sex drive as soon as a primitive knowledge of sex processes has been achieved. Here, as well, their goal is to prove their masculinity.

When birth fantasies, thoughts of castration, or analogous thoughts of being below, shortness of breath, being run over, etc., arise in the neurosis, these are neither wishes, nor repressed fantasies, but symbolically expressed fears of succumbing, against which the neurotic endeavors to safeguard himself, or which he calls to mind as a warning.

Fear of Female Dominance

A frequent type which, however, I have considered only rarely, are sons of strong-willed, masculine mothers. They are deeply imbued with a fear of the female. In their fantasies, the masculine woman—that is, the woman who wants to be on top, wants to be a man—often plays a part. Or else they have the symbolic fantasy of the *penis captivus* [vaginismus] —that is, the fear not to be able to come free from the female, borrowing the image from the intercourse of dogs. To be very careful, they exaggerate enormously. Their own sensuality appears to them gigantic, the female becomes a demon, and thus their distrust grows to the point where they become sexually incompetent. They must scrupulously test and spy on every girl (Griselda!).[18]

Again the question arises: Is what the neurotic shows us as libido, genuine? We would say, "No." His sexual prematurity is forced. His compulsion to masturbate serves his defiance and as a safeguard against the demon woman, and his love-passion only aims at victory. His love-bondage is a game that aims at not submitting to the "right" partner, and his deviating fantasies, even his active deviations, serve only to keep him away from love. They serve him, of course, as a

[18] Griselda, legendary heroine of a novel in *Decameron*, by Boccaccio (1313–75), is a poor peasant girl whose obedience and humility are most severely tested by her princely husband.

substitute, but only because he wants to play a hero role and is afraid of getting caught under the wheels if he goes the normal way. The "core problem" of the neurosis, the incest fantasy, usually has the function of nourishing the belief in one's own overpowering libido and therefore avoiding as much as possible any "real" danger.

A CASE OF SEXUALITY AS MEANS OF PERSONAL STRIVING[19]

I shall now present a case who is still in treatment. But the structure of his neurosis is clear enough that I may give excerpts as illustrations of my assertions.

The patient is a twenty-two-year-old draftsman who complained about frequent trembling of his hands for the past year and a half, and frequent nocturnal pollutions. At the age of five years he lost his father, who had become blind, and who during his last three years was hardly able to walk or even stand by himself. Not until he was seventeen years old did the patient learn that his father had died of spinal consumption, a disease supposedly caused by excessive sexual intercourse. At that time the patient had been masturbating heavily and now became very frightened about his future.

The patient had frequent occasion to fear for his future. As a little boy he was weaker and smaller than his siblings and playmates, and always sought protection from his mother, who conspicuously pampered him as the youngest child. He was always timid and shy. However, he soon insisted on having the last word and on being the first among his playmates, so that he never made friends. Soon he wanted to know everything, in sexual matters as well as in school. His ambition was to become a great man, and he was the only one of his siblings to go to high school.

The following early recollection reflects the masculine protest of his childhood. He was lying on his back in the grass

[19] Translated from A1911a as published in A1914a, 1928 ed., pp. 95–100.

and saw above, in the clouds, the picture of his father—he, the feminine weakling, in the feminine position, with his father above, in the position of the man.

Until recent years he had some feminine traits, and as a child he was often asked to take a girl's part in plays, dressed as a girl. For a long time he shared a bed with his two-years-older sister, where he satisfied his sexual curiosity. In his dreams he had occasional fantasies of incest, relating to his mother and sister.

His mother was very moralistic, and he could observe her harsh discipline toward his older brothers when they had love affairs. Regarding the marriages of her children, she was primarily concerned with material matters, and she harassed one of her daughters-in-law for many years because the daughter was poor. All in all, his mother dominated him in every respect.

Our patient had erections and masturbated from his ninth year on. Later he frequently had erections when he was in the company of girls. At the age of fourteen he began to masturbate more regularly. This spoiled any company of girls so much for him that he preferred to be alone. He became convinced that his sexual libido was immense and hardly to be coped with.

When he learned of his father's disease and had to assume that his father was as sensuous as he himself, this gave him a powerful shock, and he stopped masturbating! Frequently he let himself be carried away to kiss a girl despite his fear of an erection, but afterward avoided for a long while any place where he might meet girls.

Was his libido really as great as he assumed? Especially was it so great that he had to safeguard himself by the fear of being with girls? Certain things would speak strictly against this. He had grown up in rural circumstances and later alone at a high school where ample occasions for sexual intercourse could be found. Some girls had made sufficient advances. As mentioned, when he learned of his father's illness and its cause, he immediately stopped masturbating. Soon after, he took up normal intercourse, but not frequently, and was easily detained from it by the thought of the expense. Girls willing to accommodate him, he left after he had conquered them, for fear of not being able to get rid of them later. He imagined every woman as a demon, extremely sensuous, wanting to dominate him, and toward whom he might be weak. But he remained strong. At the same time he looked down on women, considered them inferior, distrusted them, and always attributed egotistical motives to them.

Two years ago he met a beautiful but poor girl who at first attracted him. When they were contemplating marriage he began to suffer from profuse pollutions and, with prostitutes, from premature ejaculation or impotence. At that time he also began to tremble at work, so that he could draw only with great difficulty, and to hesitate in his speech. But these symptoms occurred only after intercourse or pollution the night before.

The most obvious assumption, that he had seen his father trembling and now imitated him to scare himself, was not confirmed by the patient. But he remembered an old high school teacher who trembled and hesitated in his speech. Then our patient interpreted this as a sign of old age in people who in their youth had had too much sexual intercourse. He had also read a pamphlet that ascribed trembling and hesitating speech to pollutions.

Further information came from his thoughts about the imminent marriage. His mother would be dissatisfied; his rich relatives would look down on him; the girl would marry him only for material reasons; she was sensuous and would draw him into the ecstasy of her lust; he was sensuous himself, and the consequences of his masturbation, pollutions, and sexual relations already set in. On the basis of these arrangements he withdrew from the girl, without really knowing how he could get rid of her completely. This hesitation is the equivalent of a "No" and at the same time safeguards him from other girls.

He trembles today to remind himself of what will threaten him someday. He trembles in order to escape his basic fear of again being under the power of a woman, as he had been with his mother. He trembles in order to avoid the fate of his father or that of the old teacher. He trembles to escape the demon woman, as well as his own sensuality and that of the girl. And he trembles in order to satisfy his mother's wish, contrary to his own, not to marry this girl, and thus, in the last analysis, prove again his dependency on a woman.

This is the reason for the notion of his own excessive sensuality as well as that of the woman, for his frequent erections and pollutions. The latter happen largely because he wants and needs them, and because he continuously thinks of sexual matters in order to engineer them.

I am asking again: How should one appraise the libido of this neurotic where everything has become contrived, arranged, magnified, distorted, a purposive unnatural product, an asset and a liability at the same time?

The following dream reflects all these traits and emphasizes the most important dream tendency, that of safeguarding. "A buxom young woman sits in the nude on a sofa. I don't know what she says." He thinks of a prostitute and his senses leave him when he sees the naked woman. "She tries to seduce me." The demon woman. "I wanted to go along, but at the last moment realized that I was about to have a pollution and held myself back from her." The attempt to take a course in life without a woman. The dream as a whole is a warning against pollutions and intercourse as the exogenous factors of tabes.

The simple explanation that tabes was the result of syphilis had no effect. Only the understanding for his exaggerated safeguarding tendencies stopped the trembling.

What then is the core problem of this neurosis? The incest fantasy served only the purpose to guarantee his belief in his exaggerated, criminal fantasy. The repression of his inclination to masturbate, which was easy, was followed by an equivalent or better safeguard, the pollutions. Only when he was facing marriage and feared to be underneath again as formerly, not like the man, the father, on top, to come under the influence of a woman, and thus to be forced to admit his inferiority before everybody, did he become "sick."

Incidentally, he could tolerate as little to be subordinated to a man, be it one of his colleagues, whom he continuously depreciated and with whom he was constantly on bad terms; teachers who appeared to him in frequent examination dreams; or his superior, before whom he had on certain days his attacks of trembling.

How, then, does sexuality come into the neurosis, and what part does it play there? It is awakened early and stimulated when inferiority and a strong masculine protest exist; it is regarded and felt as gigantic so that the patient may safeguard himself in good time; or it is devaluated and eliminated as a factor if this serves the tendency of the patient. In general one cannot take the sexual impulses of the neurotic or of civilized man as genuine and count on them, let alone continue to represent them, no matter how they are viewed, as the fundamental factor of the healthy or diseased mental life. They are never causes, but always worked-over material and means of personal striving.

The true attitude toward life can be clearly seen already in the first dreams and recollections of a person. This is evidence that the recollection is construed in the sense of a planful procedure.

Our patient's earliest dream, approximately from his fifth year, was: "A bull follows me and wants to gore me." The patient believes that he had this dream shortly after the death of his father, who had been bedridden for a long time. When we establish a connection to the fantasy of the father in the clouds (God?), the thought of the boy's fear of death occurs. The later "reconstruction" (Birstein, 1913) probably took the tabes of the father and his death, which had so shocked the patient, into consideration. The bull must, further, have represented masculinity to the boy, who had grown up in the country, which showed him as the pursued one in an unmanly—that is, female—role. Even if one does not want to go that far in the interpretation, one gets the feeling that the child is filled with dark premonitions.

The second dream continues the bad expectations. He felt as if he had fallen off and landed on a hard surface. Dreams of falling always point toward a pessimistic carefulness of the dreamer, which frightens with bad possibilities, with "being underneath."

His earliest recollection was, he believes, that on the first day of school he went very fast into the girls' school and cried when he was sent off to the boys' school. We may take this as a metaphor of his desire not to be sick, miserable, dead, "underneath," like his father, but to seek the future healthy, strong, and alive, corresponding to a female role as he found it in his strong mother who, according to everyone, conducted her affairs like a man.

The hesitation [*later added:* from a lack of preparation] in his masculine role with all the pertaining, including neurotic phenomena, had become the axis of his psychological life. His sex life necessarily corresponded to this.

CRITIQUE OF REPRESSION[20]

Repression–Culture Circularity

I may presuppose in this circle a knowledge of "repression" as this has been conceived and described by Freud. The causes of repression, however, and the path from repression to neurosis are by no means as clear as is generally assumed in the Freudian school. Attempts at explanation created a very large number of auxiliary constructs, often unproven or even unprovable, not to mention those constructs that in the most obvious manner resort to analogies from physics or chemistry, such as "damming up," "increased pressure," "fixation," "flowing back into infantile paths," "projections," and "regression."

The causes of repression are conceived too summarily in the papers of this school, as dogmatically used stereotypes, but also as intuitions the bases of which are always worth determining. Regarding successful and unsuccessful repression, this problem becomes all the more mysterious if we trace it to "sexual constitution." The simple statement of repression, however, shows lack of psychological insight. The causes of "sublimation" and "substitute formation" are likewise not explained; instead, the same idea is repeated in different words.

[20] Translated from A1911b as published in A1914a, 1928 ed., pp. 100–6, with parts having appeared in A1956b, pp. 60–67.

"Organic repression" appears as merely an emergency exit, showing that changes in the modes of operation are possible; it has hardly any bearing on the theory of the neuroses. Thus the following are considered: repressed drives and drive complexes, repressed complexes, repressed fantasies, repressed experiences, and repressed wishes.

And above all this, there hovers as *deus ex machina* one magic formula–pleasure, of which Nietzsche says so well: "All pleasure wants eternity, wants deep, deep eternity" (*Zarathustra,* iii, 15). And Freud says: "Man cannot forego any pleasure he has ever experienced."

Under this assumption those drastic forms arise that every work of a disciple of Freud must show: the boy who is compelled to suckle at his mother's breast; the neurotic who seeks again and again the enjoyment of being bathed in wine or amniotic fluid; on up to the purer sphere where the man who is seeking the right girl will never find her because he is seeking the irreplaceable mother.

This way of observing represented an important methodological advance. But it lent itself to reification and freezing of the psyche which, in reality, is constantly at work and mindful of the future. The acceptance of the concept of complex was a further step toward priority of the topological over the dynamic view. Naturally, this was not carried so far that the principle of energetics, the *panta rhei* [everything is in a state of flux], could not have been brought in as an afterthought.

The real question is this: Is the driving factor in the neurosis the repression, or is it, as I should like to state it in neutral terms for the time being, the deviating, irritated psyche, in the examination of which repression can also be found?

And now I beg you to note: Repression takes place under the pressure of culture, under the pressure of the "ego drives," with the aid of thoughts of an abnormal sexual constitution, of sexual precocity.

QUESTION: Where does our culture come from?
ANSWER: From the repression.

Efforts and Attitudes Toward the Environment

And what about the "ego drives," a concept as redundant and empty as few others? Do they not have the same "libidinous" character as the sex drive? The ego drives are not rigidified and separate, but [*later added:* according to the observations of Individual Psychology] efforts and attitudes toward the environment, wanting to be significant, striving for power, for dominance, toward being above. With this understanding we must focus theoretically and practically on two possibilities: Wanting to be significant (a) may inhibit, repress, or modify certain drives, (b) must primarily have the effect of stimulating.

For us the constant factor is the culture, the society, and its institutions. The drives, whose satisfaction is actually considered as a purpose, must be relegated to the function of direction-giving means to initiate satisfactions usually in the distant future. The eye, the ear, and also the skin have acquired the peculiar ability of extending our radius of effectiveness beyond the bodily spatial sphere. Through presensitivity, our psyche steps beyond the present—that is, temporally beyond the limits of primitive drive satisfaction. Here increased efforts are as urgent as repressions, and these relationships include the necessity for an extensive safeguarding system, of which the neurosis is a small part. [*Later added:* This means that the neurosis is first of all a safeguarding device.]

These efforts begin on the first day of infancy and change all bodily and psychological tendencies to such an extent that, for example, what we see never represents anything original or primary, anything that has not been influenced, or anything that has become changed only at a later time. Instead, the adaptation of the child directs and modifies his drives until he has adapted himself in some way to the environment. In this first stage of life one cannot speak of a permanent model nor of identification when the child orients himself by a model, for this is often the only way for immediate drive satisfaction.

If we consider the varied manner and tempo in which drives have been satisfied everywhere and at all times, and how much this has depended on social institutions and economic conditions, we arrive at a conclusion that is analogous to the above, namely that drive satisfaction, and consequently the quality and strength of the drive, are at all times variable and therefore not measurable.

As noted before, from observations of the sex drive in neurotics I have come to the conclusion that the apparently libidinous and sexual tendencies of the neurotic as well as those of the normal individual in no way permit inferences regarding the strength or composition of their sex drives.

Adaptation, Obedience, and Defiance

How does the child adapt himself to a given family environment? Let us recall how diversely child organisms express themselves, even during the first months of life, when one can still gain an over-all view. Some children can never get enough to eat, others are quite moderate; some refuse changes in diet, others want to eat everything. The same is true with regard to seeing, hearing, excretion, bathing, and relations to other persons of the environment. Yet already during the first days the child feels reassured if we take him into our arms. Educational influences that smooth the way for the child are of far-reaching significance here.

Already these first adaptations contain affective values in relation to the persons of the environment. The child is reassured, feels secure, loves, obeys, etc.; or he becomes insecure, timid, defiant, and disobedient. If one intervenes early with intelligent tactics, a condition results that might be described as one of carefree cheerfulness [*later added:* forgivingness], and the child will hardly feel the coercion that is contained in every education. Mistakes in education, on the other hand, especially when the organs are insufficiently developed, lead to such frequent disadvantages and feelings of displeasure that the child seeks safeguards. By and large, two chief trends remain from this situation: oversubmissiveness, or rebellion and tendency toward independence. Obedience or defiance—the human psyche is capable of operating in either direction [see A1910d].

These direction-giving tendencies modify, change, inhibit, or excite every drive impulse to such an extent that any manifestly innate drive can be understood only from this point of view. "Fair is foul, and foul is fair," as the witches chant in *Macbeth.* Grief becomes joy, pain changes into pleasure, life is thrown away, death appears desirable—as soon as defiance interferes strongly. What the opponent loves will be hated, and what others discard will be highly valued. What culture prohibits, what parents and educators disadvise, precisely that will be chosen as the most ardently desired goal. An object or a person will attain value only if others will thereby suffer. Defiant individuals will always persecute others, yet will always consider themselves persecuted. Thus a certain greed or hasty desire arises that has one analogy only, namely the murderous struggle of all against all, the kindling of envy, avarice, vanity, and ambition in our modern society.

The tension from person to person is too great in the neurotic; his drive desire is so intensified that in restless expectation he continuously chases after his triumph. The clinging to old childhood disorders, such as thumb sucking, enuresis, nail biting, and stuttering, is to be explained in this way. In cases where these tendencies, which are only apparently libidinous, have been permanently retained, we can confidently speak of defiance.

The same holds for so-called early masturbation, sexual precocity, and premature sexual intercourse. I knew a seventeen-year-old girl from a good family who had frequent sexual intercourse from her fourteenth year on. Even so she was frigid. Whenever she quarreled with her mother, which happened regularly at brief intervals, the girl always knew how to secure sexual intercourse for herself. Another girl wet the bed after each depreciation on the part of her mother, and soiled it with feces.

Poor progress in school, forgetfulness, lack of occupational satisfaction, and sleeping compulsion are likewise phenomena of protest in the neurotic. In the fight against an opponent they are retained as valuable, I do not say, as pleasurable.

A part of this kind of psyche is described by Siegmund in Wagner's *Walkyrie:* "How many I met, wherever I found them, whether I courted a friend or a brother, I was always ostracized. Misfortune rested on me. What I considered right, others considered bad. Whatever appeared bad to me, others favored it. I got into a fight wherever I was. I met with anger wherever I moved. When I longed for bliss, I aroused but pain."

Thus develops the character of the neurotic that I have described most explicitly in "On Neurotic Disposition" (A1909a) and *The Neurotic Constitution* (A1912a).

Neurotic Striving for Significance, with Two Case Examples

Whence comes this craving for significance, the pleasure in the perverted (*Lust am Verkehrten*), this defiant clinging to errors, and these safeguarding measures against too much and too little, in which latter the patient takes recourse to self-depreciation, only to assert himself afterward, or elsewhere? (See my deliberations on pseudomasochism, A1910f.)

As you know, I have made two foci of psychological development responsible for this, which I shall mention here only briefly. The one rests in the emergence of an increased inferiority feeling, which I have always observed in connection with inferior organs. The other is a more or less distinct hint of an earlier fear of playing a feminine role. Both support the need of rebellion and the attitude of defiance to such an extent that neurotic traits will always develop, whether the individual concerned is considered well, is being treated for neurosis, or makes a name for himself as a genius or a criminal.

From this point on, feelings are falsified. We are no longer dealing with simple, natural relationships but with chasing after and grabbing presumed triumphs that seem to lie tempting in the future and that permanently fixate a diseased attitude. The neurotic lives and thinks much farther into the future than the normal individual and usually evades the present test situations. Very frequently the character traits of the neurotic are hidden. This explains why when I described them, they were considered to be rare, the peculiarities of the eccentric.

What does the neurotic say to these traits of his? Some are aware of them even if they do not recognize their extent or consequences. Many have known them once and then forgotten them out of ambition and vanity. They then safeguard themselves from this undignified egotism by a sort of opposite action. We see in such cases egotistic drive impulses of an undignified kind—for example, avarice, revenge, malice, cruelty—replaced by others, of an ethical content. Thus "the passion to be significant" must be inside, must have taken the lead!

Case 1. A good example of such drive repression is a case of stuttering that I reported in a lecture before the Philosophical Society in Vienna (see A1908e).

Stuttering is a disorder that in every point is constituted by the mechanism of the masculine protest. The patient had delivered a donation of two hundred kronen for charity purposes in the seventh district in Vienna. He was supposed to be at a distinguished restaurant in the inner city punctually, and was already very hungry. Yet he walked the whole way, ill-humored and tired as he was. He wanted to save the carfare, as it turned out during the analysis. As is the case in all neuroses, he wanted to have everything, all the money, all women, all souls, and continuously attempted to depreciate others.

He paid avid attention to his evaluation by others. He could lead an ascetic life when it would bring him recognition; he could be exceedingly studious when it was a matter of excelling others; he could be charitable when people would see it; but he was a miser in small matters when he believed nobody noticed him. When someone accomplished something, he was in bad humor; when someone was liked, he attacked. He was incessantly at odds with his father and not afraid to threaten suicide when he wanted to have his will. His stuttering was directed against his father, upset all his father's plans, and secured for our patient greater freedom of movement. At the same time, he safeguarded himself from marriage. He broke off any relationship to a girl after a while, with the explanation that as long as he stuttered he could not get married. This example of the "long love series," as Freud calls it [*later added:* and erroneously refers to the Oedipus complex], came about in reality because the patient wanted all women, like Don Juan, and was afraid of two things from which he wanted to safeguard himself: (1) that he would be dominated by a woman, be subservient to her, and would have to give up others; (2) that with his egotism (of which he was conscious, however, only in his feelings, not in his thoughts), he would be a bad husband and father, and would therefore be deceived by his wife and children as punishment.

The uncovering of these protest traits is generally the first part of analysis and is usually followed by improvement, but regularly by strong resistance, which manifests itself in attempts to depreciate the therapist.

Case 2. Another of my patients came from Hungary to be treated because, as it turned out in the analysis, he could not bear that his sister, whom I had cured, spoke well of me. You will say, he was in love with his sister. Correct! But only when she thought well of a man. At first the patient was polite, almost humble and modest, and was full of integrity and truthfulness. When I proved to him his revengefulness, malice, dishonesty, and envy, he was for a long time furious, but in the end admitted everything. But he also declared that now he would have to remain with me until he would be well, even if that would take several years. When I replied that he would remain as long as I would approve, he sat for a while in thought. Then he asked with a smile: "Has anyone yet in treatment with you committed suicide?" I replied: "Not yet, but I am prepared for it at any time." "To knock the weapon from his hand"—that is, to make the neurotic's pathological means appear ineffective—is the goal of any psychotherapeutic tactic.

This patient suffered among other things also from sleeplessness. He urged me to discuss this symptom, saying that he would be satisfied if he only could get his sleep back. The explanation went smoothly, and he fully regained his sleep. But he did not tell me about it until quite some time later.

Has then the patient repressed his character traits? Not at all. His entire masculine protest became apparent, however, in a way that he felt was not very offensive, innerly nor outwardly. But Freud describes in similar terms the result of unsuccessful repression. The traces of the repressed drive impulses can always be clearly recognized in the neurosis, an insight to which Freud himself has contributed. They can be seen not only in the fantasies of the neurotic and in his dreams, but especially through psychological analysis, which teaches us to recognize the small and great disharmonies and incongruencies in the life of the patient and permits their resolution.

Inferiority-feeling-Masculine-protest Dynamics and Onset of Neurosis

Of course, this work is still quite incomplete when we have only uncovered the neurotic character. But it is important especially because this knowledge is a warning to the patient. The more difficult part of the treatment leads then in my experience regularly to the two points of psychological development of the neurotic, to the sources of neuroses: the feeling of inferiority and the masculine protest.

But now to the main question: Through what does the neurotic become ill? When does his neurosis become manifest? Freud has paid less attention to this point. But we know that he assumes the cause to lie in an incident through which the repression is strengthened and the old psychological conflict is renewed. This certainly lacks clarity. Perhaps the present discussion will help solve the problem.

According to my experience, the neurotically disposed individual, who in fact always suffers, responds to any feeling of disparagement or even its expectation with an acute or chronic attack. This marks the time of the onset of the neurosis. New drive-repressions are only incidental phenomena that form under the accentuated pressure of the masculine protest, the urge for significance, and the safeguarding tendencies.

CASE OF SEXUALITY CONTINUED[21]

Fear of Female Superiority

I want to demonstrate the above with the first-mentioned case. Our patient remembered that he trembled for the first time while playing the violin at a time when he should have promised marriage to Albertine, the girl whom he apparently loved so much. On account of the trembling he stopped playing the violin. Now we learn the following: Albertine was an excellent pianist, so that he often thought he would like to accompany her on the violin if only he could play better. And if he married her, there might even have been a concert, in which his wife would have been definitely ahead of him. This had been the fear all his life: a wife who would be superior to him.

I have never met a neurotic who would not at least secretly have been afraid of this. From the literature I only would like to mention the case of Ganghofer, reported by Alexander Witt (1911), furthermore a quite analogous case from the memoirs of Stendhal.[22] In both cases we find childhood recollections of a woman stepping over the child. Fantasies of giant women, Walkyries, women who tie or beat boys, who at times do this in pseudomasochism; fairy tales of witches, nymphs, women with masculine genitals, with a fish tail, or similar to the childhood recollection of Leonardo da Vinci are frequent and find their equivalent and similar counterparts in the equally frequent birth fantasies, castration thoughts, and wishes for the role of a girl. This latter often appears in very mild form in the question: "What would be the feelings of a girl?"

Our patient had a similar childhood recollection, namely

[21] Translated from A1911b as published in A1914a, 1928 ed., pp. 106–9, with parts having appeared in A1956b, pp. 67–69.

[22] Pseudonym of Marie Henri Beyle (1783–1842), French novelist.

that a servant girl was above him. That means: "The woman is stronger than the man!" Early childhood recollections, like fantasies of vocational choice, always contain the person's effective outlook on life, regardless of whether the recollections are genuine, fantasied, or reconstructed (Birstein, 1913). (See A1913d.)

This early recollection of our patient was not repressed nor forgotten, but apparently completely disconnected from his present or former psychological state and thus denuded of all its significance. Had it been a causative factor? No one can assume that. From his early history, recollections appear of an energetic mother who as a widow administered her large estate, got along without a husband, and of whom people said she was like a man. This mother who pampered him, yet also punished him, was definitely superior to him.

When subsequently his yearning awakened that he, as a weakly child with feminine habitus who wet his bed and for this was often ridiculed and punished, should become a man, and when he expressed his masculine protest in thoughts, dreams, and defiant bedwetting, such recollections came to his help as that he often play-acted in feminine clothes and that on his first school day he went with his older sisters to the girls' school and refused with tears to go to the boys'. And still there were aggravations that drove him farther into the masculine protest. His pubic hair grew late, and his penis appeared shorter than those of his peers. He established his goal all the higher, wanted to accomplish extraordinary things, wanted to be the first in school, at the office, until he found Albertine, of whose superiority he was afraid.

Depreciation Tendency

Our patient had depreciated all girls and women, including his mother, in the usual way, out of fear. They were not intelligent, not independent, and were frivolous. As Hamlet says: "You jig, you amble, and you lisp, and nickname God's creatures, and make your wantonness your ignorance. Go to, I'll no more on't; it hath made me mad." Our patient additionally claimed that women smelled bad.

Olfactory component. Incidentally, Freud has repeatedly attributed to the "olfactory component" special significance as a libidinous component; but it appears more and more as a neurotic fraud. A fifty-four-year-old patient who from fear of childbirth became seriously neurotic, had toward the end of her treatment the following unambiguous dream: "I am unpacking eggs, and they all stink. I say: Phew, how they stink." The following day her husband was supposed to arrive. She had already depreciated all medical authorities in Germany and Austria.

A neurotic actress in talking about love affairs said: "I am not at all afraid of such affairs. I am actually completely amoral. There is only one thing: I have found that all men smell bad, and that violates my aesthetic sense." We will understand: With such an attitude one can well afford to be amoral without incurring any danger. (For several such cases, see A1911d.) Masculine neurotics do likewise; it is their revenge on the female.

Europeans and Chinese, Americans and Negroes, Jews and Aryans mutually reproach one another for their smell. A four-year-old boy says each time he passes by the kitchen, "It stinks." The cook is his enemy. We wish to call this phenomenon the depreciation tendency, a tendency that finds an analogy in the fable of the fox and the sour grapes.

Sexual relations. From what does the depreciation tendency originate? It originates from the fear of an injury to one's own sensitivity. It is likewise a safeguarding tendency, initiated by the urge toward significance, and is psychologically of the same rank as the wish to be above, to celebrate sexual triumphs, to fly, or to stand on a ladder, staircase, or the gable of a house (Solness in Ibsen's *The Master Builder*). One quite regularly finds in the neurotic that the tendencies to depreciate a woman and to have intercourse with her go closely together. The feelings of the neurotic express plainly: "I wish to depreciate the woman by sexual intercourse." Afterward he is likely to leave her and to turn to others. I have called this the Don Juan characteristic of the neurotic. It corresponds to Freud's "love series" (*Liebesreihe*), which he interprets in a fantastic manner.

The depreciation of women, the mother as well as all other women, causes many a neurotic to seek refuge with prostitutes (A1913g), where he spares himself the bother of depreciation, and beyond this, sees his relatives burst with fury. The boy sees or suspects that it is masculine to be on top. Usually the mother is the woman from whom he tries to establish distance. He wants to play the man toward her, to depreciate her, and to elevate himself. He may even call her names, beat or ridicule her, become disobedient and obstreperous toward her, try to boss her, etc.

Oedipus Complex or Masculine Protest?

Whether and how much libido are involved here are totally indifferent. The neurotic's masculine protest also may turn against other girls and women, usually on the path of least resistance, toward servants and governesses. Later he becomes habituated to masturbation and pollutions, combining with these safeguarding tendencies against the demon woman.

This applied also to our patient. When he could not reach his goal with his mother—namely, to be the master—he turned toward the servant girl with whom, at the age of six to seven, he had more success. He sees her in the nude and reaches under her skirts. Until the present this form of aggression was his chief sexual activity. He could have intercourse only with prostitutes—until he had to prove to himself that he could not marry. Then the pollutions and the impotence began and the fear of his enormous sexuality together with the presumed dangers of paralysis and trembling in old age. Or better: Trembling and stammering set in like pollution and impotence, because they could safeguard him from marriage.

Probably he would have broken off the relationship with Albertine in time and have been spared from neurosis if a third party had not appeared on the scene. This was too much for his pride. Now he could not give way, and yet he did not want to grasp. His "libidinous" strivings, the desire to possess Albertine, filled his consciousness completely. But the unconscious spoke a firm "No" and detained him from courtship by arranging symptoms that argued against marriage. Quite equivalent is his conscious thought: "I can marry only when I have a good job." But at the same time, symptoms developed that made a promotion impossible.

What has our patient "repressed"? Perhaps his sex drive, his libido? Of this he is so conscious that he thinks continuously of how to protect himself from it. A fantasy? His fantasy is in brief that the female is above him, is the stronger. I needed all my preparations to show him the connection between this and similar fantasies, and his neurosis. But then it turns out that this fantasy itself is only a warning, erected by the patient to obtain himself significance, even by devious paths.

Had he repressed libidinal urges toward his mother—that is, does he suffer from an Oedipus complex? I have seen many patients who have come to know their "Oedipus complex" very well, without feeling any improvement. Once one appreciates the masculine protest in the Oedipus complex, one is no longer justified in speaking of a complex of fantasies and wishes. One will then learn to understand that the apparent "Oedipus complex" is only a small part of the overpowering neurotic dynamic, a stage of the masculine protest, which in itself insignificant is, however, instructive in its context. It is a situation that must be taken symbolically and that yields the more important insights into the characterology of the neurotic, as other situations also do.

PART II

Sexuality and the Individual

3

SEXUALITY

DEVELOPMENT OF THE SEXUAL FUNCTION[1]

Because of the existing confusing, unverifiable, and misleading interpretations of the sexual function, we must start with the fundamental physiological and psychological facts. These give no reason for accepting such far-fetched views as an omnipotent sexual libido dominating the human mind and psyche. Such a distorted theory as that of Freud and, with some variations, of Jung, finds acceptance because of (a) the novelty, (b) the many troubles of the numerous persons with neurotic tendencies, (c) the open or hidden feeling of unsatisfied wishes in persons for whom wish fulfillment is the main problem of life.

Humanity—individuals and groups—have always wanted to find a universal power behind all phenomena and experiences of life. Individual Psychology, in a much broader and deeper sense, accepts instead the fact of life itself, in its explainable and unexplainable aspects. One of the first of these aspects is that all strivings, thoughts, feelings, characteristics, expressions, and symptoms aim toward a successful solution of social tasks.

The large number of failures in love and marriage are like all other failures due to lack of preparation. We do not recog-

[1] Reprinted with some editing from A1945b, except for the last section. Original date of paper unknown. A1945b has also been reprinted as A1964a, pp. 219–23.

nize a sexual object. Love and marriage are a task of two equal human beings forming a unit, which can be rightly solved only if these persons are trained for sufficient social interest.

Individual Psychology rejects the view that individual wishes, or the bad results of their repression, are the main problems of life. Such a concept betrays the self-centered nature of a person, as it is often seen in pampered children. It is equally unconstructive to hold to the heritage of our ancestors, who in some ways had not reached the present, still not sufficient, degree of social interest. These authors probably turn their glances to heredity and ancestors because they are satisfied to indulge in some inherited possessions rather than making an effort to use these possessions for new contributions to the welfare of humanity, for an increase in social interest.

Social Adaptation of Functions

So far as we can see, a human being is human, and is rightly called so, because he possesses by heredity all the potentialities needed for coping with social problems. But in order to cope he must develop himself physically and mentally as much as possible. The main question that arises now is: For what? For what goal must the individual strive and develop his inherited human potentialities? Individuals and humanity as a whole use their potentialities, gifts of our ancestors, for increasing these gifts in a world changed by human beings for the benefit of the whole human family. This has been done, of course, only so far as the level of social interest allowed. In addition, we must understand that all problems of life can be solved adequately only by a sufficient degree of social interest.

All human functions—brought into the world by the newborn child as potentialities for development in a social environment—must be adapted to the demands of the outside world. Eating, looking, hearing, making sounds, and moving become more and more adapted to the achievement of this goal.

All human functions are in the beginning of life in a state of confusion and automatic, and are only slowly directed toward interplay with others and with the environment. Gradually the creative power of the child accepts the challenge of the outside world, absorbs experiences, and responds to them in a way that he deems successful for taking part in the surrounding social life. His way of eating becomes proper; his ways of looking, hearing, touching, and moving prove his willingness to co-operate more or less. His thinking and talking contain more and more common values and common sense. His functions of excretion are, or should be, in agreement with the social form of his environment. Thumb sucking, nail biting, etc., being unsocial actions and sources of infections, will cease if the child accepts the social rules of the game of his environment. If they do not, the reason is always that the child has not found the way toward social culture and is striving for a personal goal of superiority.

Primary Sexual Phase

The sexual function is certainly inherited and shows itself, in the beginning, in a higher degree of the tickling sensation. Expanding, along with all the others, it leads to turgescence, erections, and concomitant feelings through automatic impulses. Touching and the resulting pleasurable tickling sensation lead to early repetition of the act, the more so if the child, as a whole, likes to go his own way and is more inclined toward wish fulfillment than toward co-operating, as is the case with the pampered child.

In that way the right co-operation is deferred until a much later time, and the child is compelled to remain at the primary phase of the sexual function. Until he has reached the right age for making the sexual function a task for two persons of different sexes—the secondary, social phase of the sexual function—only autoeroticism in its many forms is available.

In the primary phase, the usual course is masturbation. The social feeling of humanity has been and always will be opposed to this because in its hidden thinking and knowing humanity wants the secondary phase to be developed. But there is a discrepancy between the gradual development of the secondary phase, and the strong opposition toward letting children perform it on account of the dangers involved and the necessity to permit it only to physically and mentally mature boys and girls. This creates for younger children an insoluble situation. Not only parents and teachers and dangerous, stupid books and remarks increase the conflicts in the mind of the child, but his social interest, gained in the first three years, also counteracts autoeroticism. Physicians and clergymen agree more and more that the primary phase cannot be entirely avoided, that it is a natural development and should not be treated harshly, and that it does not harm the child physically or mentally.

During this primary phase one can see the power of the social interest. Remorse and diversions are common and willingly accepted. Also the frequency diminishes. But the pampered and greedy child, not able to resist any temptation, is in a worse state and often uses autoeroticism for other purposes —to abuse the attention of the parents, to entice other children, or as an alibi for defeats in school or later life.

Varieties of Autoeroticism

Later, in their distress, children often turn to other varieties of masturbation, such as indulging in erotic fantasies, using erotic pictures and other means of incitement, and sometimes another child. This opens the way to so-called homosexuality, which is only one of the many varieties of masturbation, often found among egocentric, vain adults who cling to the primary, autoerotic phase of the sexual function.

The problem of the so-called natural development of sexuality is not as simple as, for example, psychoanalysis teaches; for whatever might be assumed as the normal, natural development of sexuality cannot take place when the external circumstances stipulate a compulsory development. Keep in mind that no childhood offense is considered as serious and punished as severely as development toward the sexual norm. To be sure, when children behave in any childish, unnatural sexual way, one is not disposed in a friendly way toward them, and they are usually punished. But there is immeasurable horror when a child behaves in the normal sexual way. Thus what we observe in children again and again must be regarded as influenced by external circumstances. We do not know what development sexuality would take if we would not, and would not have to, set up barriers against it.[2]

Certain types who show sexual stimulation when irritated or fearful (as others respond with heart palpitations or intestinal or bladder troubles) indulge in sadistic or masochistic daydreams and night dreams. This type may later become a complete failure in his sexual function by developing the deviation of sadism or masochism.

All the other deviations—fetishism, sodomy, necrophilia, etc.—are varieties of the primary sexual phase. They probably always betray the misconception and the style of life of a pampered or neglected child who has not grown up to a degree of social interest sufficient for full co-operation with others. This is also true of persons who are promiscuous, masturbators, or exclusive frequenters of prostitutes.

The neurotic symptoms of sexual dysfunction, impotence, frigidity or vaginismus, and premature ejaculation also betray the primary phase of sexuality. This phase has not been overcome because of lack of social interest.

Secondary Sexual Phase

Love as a task of two equal persons of different sexes calls for physical and mental attraction, exclusiveness, and a total and final surrender. The right solution of this task of two persons is the blessing of socially interested (adjusted) persons

[2] This paragraph translated from A1928c, pp. 5–6.

who have proved their right attitude by having friends, being prepared for a useful job, and showing mutual devotion.

Expression of the Life Style[3]

Many psychologists believe that the development of sexuality is the basis for the development of the whole mind and psyche, as well as for all the physical movements. In the view of the present writer, this is not true. Rather, the entire form and development of sexuality depend on the personality–the style of life and the prototype.[4]

In childhood, matters are complicated by the psychological relations with the parents. Poor sexual training is incidental to psychological conflict between child and parent. A fighting child, especially during adolescence, may abuse sexuality with the deliberate intention to hurt the parents. Boys and girls have been known to have sex relations just after a fight with their parents. Children take these means of revenging themselves on their parents, particularly when they see that the parents are sensitive in this regard.

The sexual drive should be harnessed to a useful goal in which all of our activities are expressed. If the goal is properly chosen, neither sexuality nor any other manifestation of life will be overstressed. . . . In a normal style of life, sex will find its proper expression. This does not mean that we can overcome neuroses, the marks of an erroneous style of life, merely by free sexual expression. The belief, so widely propagated, that repressed libido is the cause of neurosis is false. Rather . . . neurotic persons do not find their proper sexual expression.

One meets persons who have been advised to give more free expression to their sex instincts and who have followed this advice, only to make their condition worse. The reason . . . is that such persons fail to harness their sexual life with

[3] Reprinted from A1929d, pp. 125–26, 128, 129–30.

[4] By "prototype" Adler (A1929d) means the rudimentary, formative precursor of the adult life style, the "model of a matured personality" (pp. xvii–xviii).

a socially useful goal, which alone can change their neurotic condition. The expression of the sex instinct by itself does not cure the neurosis, for it is a disease in the life style, if we may use the term, and it can be cured only by ministering to the style of life.

WOMAN'S ATTITUDE TOWARD SEXUALITY[5, 6]

There is no firm basis for studying woman's attitude toward sexuality. According to present-day scientific trends, one should study blood composition, draw conclusions from the endocrine glands and their correlates, and assume that the proper physical conditions would result in ideal sexual behavior.

But by what ideal do we judge? Does the goal of woman's sexual development depend solely on the adequacy of her procreative glands? How do we judge good or bad? Are we looking for the greatest happiness, the largest progeny, or full satisfaction of the drives? Do we demand equal value of the two sexes, or the subordination of one to the other? As many questions, as many goals of women's development, so many demands for sexual forms of life! The literature on this most human problem is vast.

More illuminating than the scientific writings, followed by a flood of pseudoscientific absurdities, are the works of poets, novelists, painters, and sculptors. We find that beginning with the Bible and myths and fairy tales, up to modern short stories and plays and the lyrical poetry of men and women, the erotic problem is dealt with and elaborated on. But since art, like science, has so far been almost exclusively the work of men, it reflects primarily man's knowledge of the female soul. Often important problems remain unsolved, reminding us of

[5] Translation of A1926e, as reprinted in A1930d, pp. 89–97.

[6] General references: G. Heymans (1910), Otto Weininger (1918), Vaerting (1923), J. S. Mill (1869), Schirmacher (1905), Ellen Key (n.d.), Paul Moebius (1903), Johann Bachofen (1861), Bernhard Aschner (1924), Wilhelm Liepmann (1922), Hugo Sellheim (1924), Helene Deutsch (1925). [Author's note.]

the confession of old and new riddle guessers that "woman is a riddle."

The masculine preponderance among these opinions is certainly an evil, often reducing woman to an object for male or female drives. Woman's task is generally seen as to be beautiful and to bear children. Moreover, striking deficiencies in character, intellectual freedom, objective striving, and aptitude for vocation and public life are so emphasized that woman's existence is justified almost entirely by love and the care of progeny. This judgment strongly influences women. They usually accept it and appear to submit to the role assigned to them by men. In exaggerated revolt, George Sand lacerates this system with the words: "The virtue of women—that is a good invention of men!"

This suggests that, besides the physical foundations, other factors affect woman's sexual attitude that modify the course of eroticism much more. Among these are the attitude of the culture, the relative number of women, and the great influence of the man due to his prerogative of active courting, his firmer economic basis, and his better schooling and training. As far as we can see, the education of girls for the role of a woman takes these factors always into account and tries to attain an adjustment to them. An attitude toward sexuality based exclusively on physique, a sexuality isolated from all other factors, can be found, if at all, only among the feeble-minded. In all other cases every form of sexuality is based on a preconceived, preparatory attitude toward the love problem.

Individual Perspective

One thing is certain: Female sexuality is by no means uniform and depends on various factors. Granted, a certain uniformity can be noted at different times and locations, with different peoples and ages, similar to fashions. Yet all semblance of uniformity notwithstanding—"Their everlasting aches and groans, in thousand tones, have all one source, one mode of healing" [as the Devil says in Goethe's *Faust*][7]—it is nevertheless evident that each individual case is quite different; for example, from the general wish to find a husband one may not conclude that there is a desirable, because socially necessary, sexual readiness. The restriction of woman's action circle, tradition, personal pride, and economic reasons urge the choice of a partner as much as do sexual impulses. Despite their organic foundation, sexual impulses are guided and changeable according to the individual's form of life and her true ultimate intentions, and can be trained in the most diverse directions. The traces of the sex drive from early childhood are modeled by the surrounding culture, and are like all other drives tamed or incited by individually comprehended experiences that are not limited to the field of sexuality. When a girl's education as a whole leads her to a definitely passive attitude toward life, her erotic behavior will also be passive.

Only in the individual case are we able to determine all these influences that have affected the sexual expression of a woman. In psychological forms of expression, such as a woman's attitude toward sexuality, one cannot expect a real causality. All organic feelings and impulses, as well as all experiences, pass through the filter of the personality and are comprehended from an individual perspective. From the viewpoint of an ideal type, every utilization of the above factors, every self-evaluation and its effect, are developed in a more or less mistaken manner. A woman will experience and evaluate the approach, courtship, inward and outward habitus of a partner according to her goal for her way of life.

All so-called "feminine" traits are extremely subject to the social balance of forces between men and women, owe their origin to it, and may be shaped and destroyed by it. Even apparently innate traits, such as waiting for a suitor, passivity, reserve, feminine modesty, motherliness, and monogamy are subject much more than is realized to the trend of the times, and are directed by the final goal [of the individual]. Hints at

[7] Part 1, Scene IV, Bayard Taylor translation of the original, *"Es ist ihr ewig Weh und Ach aus einem Punkte zu kurieren."*

exhibitionism, usually justified by fashion, must be evaluated as neutral; while more explicit forms probably disclose a more active character.

In connection with this and the depreciation of the partner one frequently finds a fetishistic overestimation of unimportant matters. This often limits the love choice as severely as an ideal picture of the partner. Against both of these demands and still others, any perfection may fail. Often they are only poorly understood pretenses to preclude any choice. Otherwise the love choice, always corresponding to a self-limitation of the sexual drive and its superstructure, may follow the most varied motives. The impressions of early childhood, the image of the father, a brother, or one's own people are often highly codetermining. The choice of the love partner, as long as it is free, will always correspond wholly to the peculiarities, defects, and advantages of the personal attitude. A straightforward feeling of strength, rarely found, will give preference to similar men. Girls secretly seeking superiority often feel attracted to weaklings, or cripples, or choose below their status. Similarly, the choice of someone close at hand, or a relative, points to a feeling of weakness, as does the preference for much older or much younger men. Often a motherly trend is strengthened in a most unfruitful manner, aiming at the salvation or elevation of a fallen partner and attempting to repress the regularities of normal sexuality.[8]

Favorable and Unfavorable Factors

Eroticism is never mere animal sex drive, never, as Schopenhauer believed, merely an allurement of nature for the purpose of procreation of the human race. It is rather a highly qualified part of the human social feeling that reflects the entire personality and thus also the degree of the connectedness with the social life and the preparation for a life for two.

The development of the ability to love is advanced by cer-

[8] This and the preceding paragraph are inserted from pp. 95–96.

tain conditions, threatened by others. The situation in childhood is decisive, as well as the early decision by the girl regarding her future role as a woman.

Belief in her own strength, an optimistic view of the future, the ability to make contact with people, the inclination to spread joy, an uncritical feeling of belonging to the female sex, and respect for the feminine role are always favorable elements.

Ignorance of her own feminine role or hesitation during several years of childhood, strong attachment to one single person in the family, general feelings of weakness and inferiority, being raised without love, lack of confidence in herself and others, ugliness but also beauty, and especially contempt of womanhood can under any circumstances disturb the preparation for love.

Unfavorable Development

The situation of a girl in childhood is of the greatest importance. A bad marriage of the parents, rudeness, drunkenness and recklessness of the father, or open unfaithfulness cause daughters to fear for the rest of their lives that they may meet the fate of their miserable and deeply humiliated mother. Even when they have the best sexual constitution, their attitude toward men will never be free from distrust, scruples, and inhibitions. Their goal and final purpose will be to avoid the degradation that they presume to be a certainty in the feminine role, and will force them to exclude that role. This brings into their whole life and attitude toward men a system of safeguards in the form of inhibitions, nervous symptoms, and sexual deviations.

In line with this, their view of the world, their logic, habits, and training of the sex drive—in fact, their entire course of life—are forced into a direction away from men. Depending on the personality, which begins to develop in the first years of childhood, the experiences, and the more or less mistaken perspective, the natural, ultimate goal of eroticism changes into a substitute goal (*Ersatzziel*). This substitute goal (A1917a, p. 281) always lies in the field of secondary matters (sexual deviations of all kinds and accentuation of some sexual details), or it fulfills only a part of sexuality (frigidity), brings fear of men, indifference, or aversion, or a masculine tendency, and leads to a masculine role in sexual life, as well as in the woman's whole *modus vivendi*.

Such partial or total turning away from the feminine role has characteristic expressions. Frequently we find aversion to having children and nursing them; but then again, in milder cases, the child may become the exclusive ultimate purpose, in contrast to the husband. In most cases nervous symptoms of all kinds prevent a harmonious development of eroticism. Inclination toward prostitution and exaggerated polygamous tendencies are also manifestations of the aversion to the feminine role. Vaginismus is also a telling expression of this rejection.

All these manifestations that detract from the feminine role have in common girls' dissatisfaction with their social position in the culture. This is nurtured by the real or apparent preponderance of men, and the resulting belligerent attitudes of women, which may range from open revolt to dull submission. The urge to change this situation causes all ideals of government by women and emancipation, and degenerates in personal life into a hundred forms of the "masculine protest." Kant (1798), in his *Anthropologie,* points to the same experience. And Herder,[9] in his collection of bride songs of all times and peoples, found generally only sad songs.

Also, the commonly held superstition of women's inferiority, the almost complete exclusion of women from highest achievements in science and art—due partly to inadequate preparation, partly to masculine development of artistic forms of expression—generally result in embitterment and early discouragement, while only in dancing and acting women often reach the highest peaks. No wonder that the dissatisfaction with the feminine role frequently leads to an imitation of men —in fashion, wishes and fantasies, conduct of life, and erot-

[9] Johann G. von Herder (1744–1803), German philosopher, poet, and critic.

icism. No wonder that, according to the estimates of experienced physicians, approximately 70 per cent of women are frigid in spite of perfect sexual constitutions.

Along with all these reasons against free development of sexuality in the direction of a social, cultural form of expression, and usually inseparably connected with them, there is an inadequate or poor preparation for love, a serious obstacle to sexual harmony. The prevailing mutual distrust, the exaggerated self-seeking, the urge to outdo one's partner, and the fear of being inferior to him hinder spontaneous devotion and poison the love relationship. Girls who are not so pretty fear a quick cooling-off of the husband, while beautiful women feel oppressed, believing themselves merely sexual objects, and find their human dignity insulted. This is often aggravated by the partner's bachelor habits, poor handling of intercourse, or a misunderstanding of male sexuality. Awkwardness, brutality, or injuries to psychological sensitivity during the first relations may lead to permanent upset. Jealous limitations of freedom of movement at the beginning of the marriage, and impregnation contrary to agreement or against the wish of the wife may have the same effect. Fear-arousing experiences in childhood, and prejudices regarding pain and the dangers of being a woman further increase the inferiority feeling.

Sexual Disorders

The development of the sex drive urges the individual, in the course of awakened impulses, toward autoerotic masturbatory actions. Thus, sooner or later, through seduction or on her own, partly inhibited and partly encouraged by the environment and the culture, the child will happen upon masturbatory satisfactions. Harmless in themselves, they may give rise to a training toward autoeroticism that impedes the development of normal eroticism and its effects, and considerably strengthens the arguments against it because, like an ever-ready valve, it can reduce sexual tension at any time.

This view is in sharp contrast to that of the "somaticists." For us, cultural difficulties and errors, poor guidance and inadequate preparation are in the foreground, whereas those who emphasize the constitution either attribute little importance to these factors or look at them as reactions to glandular deficiencies. Against this we would stress:

1. Even the best-endowed organism may go wrong through errors and mistakes.
2. In some respect, the inferiority of organs, including the endocrine glands, appears sufficiently taken into account in our view, although always within a more important context than the purely organic. This context consists in the relationship of the inferiority to the requirements of the respective culture, and how it influences the self-esteem, leading to a low self-evaluation.
3. The physical and psychological training that ensues from woman's antisocial sexual attitude brings out still other valuations and interests, and always also changes secondarily the organic basis of the sexual function. From this curtailment further difficulties arise. The stimuli from the external world that encourage the function are warded off, impulses from the organ are stopped or postponed, and the organ is artificially put at rest and may be injured still further by the forced change in the way of life. In the "hunger strike" [anorexia nervosa] of girls, for example, which is perhaps always initiated by the "masculine protest" in rejection of the feminine role, the substances of the procreative and other endocrine glands dwindle in the course of the extreme emaciation. But even before this, sex is psychologically excluded, in that the psychological apparatus is filled with interests in nourishment and evacuation.

Lesbian love, persistence in sexual fantasies, masturbation, and pollutions are signs of masculine protest and disclose a fear of men and their rejection. Homosexual dreams are not proof of homosexuality, as is generally and prejudicially assumed, but signs of a training in a wrong direction. Desire for polygamy, exaggerated flirting, passion to compromise oneself, fantasies of being a kept woman, and exaggerated and repulsive clamoring for a man all point beyond themselves to an attempt to exclude marriage. Adultery is always the sign of a revolt against the husband, an act of revenge that is always disguised through purposefully incited eroticism.

The first menstruation often gives the signal for the outbreak of the fight against the feminine role, when there is inadequate preparation. Frequently the resistance flames up anew each time. Pain without organic causes seems to be produced by arbitrary contractions, by slowing up the blood discharge, and to arise from dissatisfaction with and rejection of the event. This view is supported by the fact that often after marriage, when there is a far-reaching reconciliation with the feminine role, the pain disappears. The widely held opinion that the menses imply impurity or sickness, often also advanced by physicians, lowers the self-confidence of women and often produces strong feelings of depression. Heightened sexual feelings (perhaps also because they are not dangerous then) are frequent during this period.

The approach of the menopause and the menopause itself become extremely difficult times for women who see in youth and beauty almost the only value of a woman. They lose the last remainder of belief in their own value. Depressed and desperate, they often try to regain a feeling of worth by increasing demands on their environment. Others plunge into destructive conflicts through their eroticism, which does not disappear at that time but is everywhere rejected, ridiculed, and not taken seriously.

Conclusion

An erroneous attitude toward life works against men and women. While we do take the organic foundations of eroticism fully into account, we must assert that the individual attitude is decisive for the erotic direction and shortcomings.

If we should name the preconditions for a woman's healthy attitude toward sex (*Sexualleben*) that are usually not met sufficiently, they would be:

1. Early enlightenment regarding the unalterability of the sexual role and reconciliation to it.

2. Educational preparation for love in accordance with social interest.
3. Respect for the feminine role.
4. Affirmation of life and of human society.

MAN'S PSYCHOSEXUAL ATTITUDE[10, 11]

Man's psychosexual attitude essentially coincides with that of women. We always measure against an ideal type of man that we envision, and ultimately sense the differences from it in terms of fitness for human living together, and for a man and a woman living together. Also, our evaluation of the uniqueness of a man depends absolutely on these presuppositions.

The difference between the sexes is that our culture has conceded to men, tacitly or openly, privileges in love life that it seeks to deny to women. Man's greater sphere of activity in love life is primarily determined by his greater sphere of activity in life altogether, but is made much easier for him because he remains free from pregnancy as a consequence of sexuality, because of his role of active courting, and because of tradition, an enormous force. In a certain accord with this there is additionally the easy master morality of men to whom the commonly accepted sexual morality does not set such narrow limits as it does to women.

Early Development

The male sexual impulse manifests itself in various intensities, usually long before puberty, and can veer into various wrong directions during boyhood, puberty, or later. Thus the attitude of a man toward the problems of life will always

[10] Original translation of A1926f, as reprinted in A1930d, pp. 98–102, 105.

[11] General references: Wilhelm Fliess (1906), Tandler and Gross (1913), Otto Weininger (1918), Magnus Hirschfeld (n.d.), Robert Müller (1907), Havelock Ellis (1912a), Hermann Rohleder (n.d.), Sigmund Freud (1923), Alfred Adler (A1912a). [Author's note.]

influence his sexual development as well. This is all the more understandable since there is no fixed measure of the sex drive, and its expressions can be increased or reduced through various influences.

Already during boyhood, these influences and the psychological direction assert themselves most clearly. The sexual preparation consists first of all in the strengthening of an adequate boy's role, in a growing understanding of the sexual problem, and in a courageous goal-setting in the direction of love and marriage. Our culture and its institutions take over a part of the work from those who are responsible for the child's upbringing. Different dress, different games, and different educational measures attempt to steer the course of development correctly. The surrounding life, analogies from animals, educational measures, and usually enlightenment by peers advance the insight into the sexual secret; reading, theater, motion pictures, and often also seduction complete this enlightenment. Since furthermore everywhere in his life a boy comes across the facts of love and marriage, since all educational measures also envision a social solution of the love and marriage problem in the future, and since the growing sexual drive seeks such a solution, the boy's world picture of the future develops in this sense.

A boy's attitude toward the other sex is at first usually one of hostility and superiority. Furious aversion against feminine dress, let alone the insinuation of being a girl, are often to be taken as an exaggerated sign of finding one's sexual role. Also, in the later boyhood years, the feeling of superiority usually comes to light, even in coeducation, and equality is denied to the girls, as if it were an obligation to do so. "The boy proudly tears himself away from the girl."[12] In the midst of this critical gesture, we often find traits of affection and being in love. Often already in the fourth, fifth, and sixth year, friendly tendencies—or those of a critical and malicious nature—appear. An inclination to tease, also to attack, is not infrequent.

[12] From Schiller's poem *Die Glocke: "Vom Mädchen reisst sich stolz der Knabe."*

The sex drive may give occasion for masturbation during the very first years. Through seduction we find sometimes in early childhood mutual masturbation or, especially in slums, normal sexual intercourse. It is also noteworthy that for boys during their development it is much easier to turn through mutual masturbation to homosexuality than to turn to normal sexual behavior.

Puberty

The fourteenth year usually brings in boys the decisive turn toward masturbation, from which they sooner or later free themselves. In puberty, the throttled sexual drive vents itself in more or less frequent pollutions. Fatigue and looking badly during this period come almost always from fear of sickness or from some disturbances in development. Masturbation and pollutions of this period can be completely overcome. If they persist for many years, they must be taken as attempts to exclude women.

During puberty and shortly thereafter, an image of the ideal girl is usually formed that is likely to show the traits of a close person. This ideal image is often subject to change later, as other ideals also often dissolve. Often there is fear of sullying this image, or a girl who embodies it, through sensual thoughts. At the same time, the most extravagant fantasy images may occur. Frequently masturbation represents the temptation to transpose sensual desire into reality.

Alongside this purity of sentiment, one often finds the desire for coarse sensuality, or the engaging in sexual relations, following the line of least resistance, usually with prostitutes or servant girls. Both are ready outlets that permit bypassing the way to love and marriage, sometimes permanently. Toward both these erroneous ways young men are often encouraged by trained and untrained educators. To close these paths will be possible only for those who do not defend the absolute necessity of early sexual relations, but are also not afraid to grant full rights to a true love where both partners are prepared to stand up for each other.

Customs and practices of society, gatherings, dances, and projects in which both sexes take part, promote and encourage the inclination toward girls that has by now developed. The training for union is a continuous, ongoing process. In thoughts, on the street, in the theater, in pictorial representations there are constant stimulations that help the inclination toward love and marriage to prevail. Marriage is, of course, to a high degree connected with economic and vocational problems. Up to that point, there is a relatively long period during which all too many youths lapse into sexual waywardness or venereal diseases.

Marriage

When a man enters marriage, he is not only faced with the categorical demands of marriage (A1925b), almost always he brings into marriage his individual requirements as well, which many times have no place there and disturb the relationship. The new situation will be a touchstone of his preparation for marriage. His preparation will always reflect his world philosophy and his attitude toward women. His choice of a mate has already been guided by his ideal requirements of a woman and of marriage.

Depending on whether a man was satisfied with his mother and sister, or could assert himself against them, the girl of his choice will be mentally and physically similar to them, or different. If he is a man who longs for warmth, he will associate with girls from whom he expects to be pampered. If he loves to prevail in a contest, he will seek girls who appear strong to him; or else he will prefer those who by their nature, stature, and strength appear easily guidable to him. Naturally, this will lead to many mistakes, primarily because no girl will tolerate permanent subjugation.

If one is properly trained for marriage, the further course of the marriage and of his sexual attitude will depend entirely on the partner. If she also knows how to create harmony, the two will be the picture of harmonious sexuality until the end of their lives. This may be a rare case, proof of the inadequate education of our progeny for marriage. Closely connected with sexuality, in such cases the feeling of unconditional comradeship will develop, so that disagreeable differences are out of the question or are easily overcome. There will also be enough room in such marriages for the new generation, who will be accepted into the same comradeship. The sexual problem will find a common solution, will not be felt as the dictation of the other, and neither party will feel like an object. The sexual belongingness (*Zugehörigkeit*) will not be troubled by anything until it slowly expires in late years, often beyond the sixtieth year. Sexual intercourse will evidence no shortcomings, nor give cause for bad humor, exhaustion, or sadness.

It is different with those who are ill prepared. In the new situation following puberty, the time of the possible and even desired sexuality, their inadequate preparation will make itself painfully felt under all circumstances, without they themselves being able to give an account. A feeling of insecurity, or inadequate self-confidence, leads one to see in sexuality, and thus in woman and in devotion to her, greater or lesser threats to one's own sphere of significance. Such individuals will lack the straightforwardness that is a main requirement for healthy eroticism. In their behavior they will show detours and deviations, the strongest of which are homosexuality and autoeroticism. Similarly, all other displacements of the sexual role, such as fetishism, sadism, masochism, and perverted mannerisms, reveal to us the old insecurity and the attempt to put private satisfaction of desires in place of those offered by society, in order thus to avoid a test of one's own worth. The choice of prostitutes and the preference for easily dissolved attachments without consequences reveal the same weakness. When we understand this dynamic correctly, we can readily appraise in a Don Juan and in cases of polygamy the lack of courage that characterizes those who do not want to see anything through and prefer to reach for cheap successes. Sexuality is "twosomeness" (Nietzsche), the achievement of two equal partners. There is no place in love for the striving of one partner to stand out at the expense of the other, to satisfy his vanity. This is an abuse, a rudeness; it blasts the structure of eroticism because it does not reckon with the laws of love.

Conclusion

Thus we come to the conclusion that the kind and degree of sexual behavior in man, as in woman, are derived from his personality, generally reflect his activity, and, as long as his sexual organs are approximately intact, are a result of his preparation and training.

SEX EDUCATION AND PUBERTY

Sex Education[13]

The subject of sex education has been frightfully exaggerated in recent times. Many people are, if we may say so, insane on the subject. They want it at any and all ages, and play up the dangers of sexual ignorance. But if we look back on our own past and that of others, we do not find such great difficulties and dangers as they imagine.

The biological difference. A child should be told at the age of two that he or she is a boy or a girl. It should also be explained at that time that one's sex can never be changed, and that boys grow up to be men and girls grow up to be women. If this is done, then the lack of other knowledge is not so dangerous. If it is brought home to the child that a girl will not be brought up like a boy nor a boy like a girl, then the sex role will be fixed in the mind, and the child will be sure to develop and to prepare for his or her role in a normal manner. If the child believes, however, that through a certain trick he or she can change sex, then trouble will result.

Trouble will also result if the parents are always expressing a desire to change the sex of a child. In *The Well of Loneliness* (Radcliffe Hall) we find an excellent literary presen-

[13] Reprinted in slightly edited form from A1930a, pp. 221–26.

tation of this situation. Parents too often like to bring up a girl like a boy or vice versa. They will photograph their children dressed in the clothes of the opposite sex. It sometimes happens, too, that a girl looks like a boy, and then people begin calling the child by the wrong sex. This may start a great confusion, which can very well be avoided.

Equal worth of the sexes. Any discussion about the sexes that tends to undervalue the female sex, and to regard boys as superior, should be avoided. Children should be made to understand that both sexes are of equal worth. This is important not merely to prevent an inferiority complex among the members of the undervalued sex, but also to prevent bad effects among the male children. If boys were not taught to think that they are the superior sex, they would not look upon girls as mere objects of desire. Nor would they look upon the relationship of the sexes in an ugly light if they knew their future tasks.

In other words, the real problem of sex education is not merely explaining to children the physiology of sexual relationships; it also involves the proper preparation of the whole attitude toward love and marriage. This is closely related to the question of social interest. If a person is not socially interested, he will make a joke of the question of sex and look at things entirely from the point of view of self-indulgence. This happens, of course, all too often, and is a reflection of the defects of our culture. Women have to suffer because in our culture it is much easier for a man to play the leading role. But the man also suffers because by this fictitious [spurious] superiority he loses touch with the underlying values.

The physical phase. As regards the physical phase of sex education, it is not necessary that children receive this education very early in life. One can wait until the child becomes curious, until he wants to find out certain things. A mother and father who are interested in their child will also know when it is proper for them to take the lead if the child is too shy to ask questions. If the child feels that his father or mother are comrades, he will ask questions, and then the answers must be given in a manner proper to his understanding.

One must avoid giving answers that stimulate the sex drive.

In this connection it may be said that one need not always be alarmed by apparently premature manifestations of the sex instinct. Sex development begins very early—in fact, in the first weeks of life. It is wholly certain that an infant experiences erogenous pleasures, and that he sometimes seeks to stimulate the erogenous zones artificially. We should not be frightened if we see signs of the beginnings of certain nuisances, but we should do our best to put a stop to these practices without seeming to attach too much importance to them. If a child finds out that we are worried over these matters, he will continue his habits deliberately in order to gain attention. It is such actions that make us think he is a victim of the sex drive, when he is really exploiting a habit as a tool for showing off. Generally little children try to gain attention by playing with their genital organs because they know that their parents are afraid of this practice. It is much the same psychology as when children play sick because they have noticed that when they are sick they are more pampered and more appreciated.

If one avoids all forms of premature stimulation, one need not have any fears. One needs only to speak at the right time in a few simple words, never irritating the child and always giving answers in a true and simple manner. Above all, one must never lie to a child, if one wants to retain his trust. If the child trusts the parent, he will discount the explanations he hears from his peers—perhaps 90 per cent of mankind get their sexual knowledge from peers—and will believe what the parent says. Such co-operation, such camaraderie is much more important than the various subterfuges that are used in the belief that they answer the situation.

Summary. These remarks sum up the most important items in the matter of sex education. We see here, as in all other phases of education, the dominant importance of the sense of co-operation and friendliness within the family. With this co-operation present, and with an early knowledge of the sex role and of the equality of man and woman, the child is well prepared for carrying on his work in a healthy manner.

Phenomena of Puberty[14, 15]

Puberty is so striking due to its physical as well as the psychological maturation processes. These begin and end in girls somewhat earlier than in boys. Physical maturation concerns all organs and takes place even when the sex glands are impaired or lost, only that then the secondary sex characteristics are inadequately developed. Psychological maturation can be temporarily or permanently hindered through inappropriate or inadequate education.

Dual aspect of puberty. Poets, researchers, and common sense have been impressed primarily by two forms of expression that permit a dual point of view. On the one hand we note increased capability, which points to qualitatively and quantitatively increased powers. These include social and occupational integration, the ability of abstract thinking, the tendency to seek a complement, the impulse toward social and sexual union, discovery or strengthening of the self, formation of a life plan, and entrance into occupational areas. Also, the tendency toward idealism, development of a life philosophy, conquest of the inner world, idealization and spiritualization of sexuality, and taking an attitude toward the values of life are often noted. All these manifestations stand out palpably when the criteria of childhood are applied to the maturing youth of thirteen to twenty-one years.

On the other hand, if one applies the criteria of the adult to this period, its shortcomings become more striking. Awkwardness and clumsiness, caused by inadequate familiarity with the organs of movement, which have now become larger and stronger; occasional timidity and shyness in unaccustomed situations; defiance, and critical and skeptical behavior; often also exaggerated striving for significance; ecstasy, fasci-

[14] Original translation of A1926g, as reprinted in A1930d, pp. 85–89.

[15] General references: Charlotte Bühler (1923), G. Stanley Hall (1918), Eduard Spranger (1925), Otto Tumlirz (1924), Alfred Adler (A1920a). [Author's note.]

nation, exuberance, an intoxication with phrases and slogans, as if thereby one would succeed in solving the riddles of life; a disparaging attitude toward previously accepted values; opposition and resistance on principle against compulsion and directed also against cultural values—all these characterize this phase. It also includes deviations and excesses of all sorts, which break through as protest and open or secret revolt against the inferiority feeling from childhood.

Thus life during puberty seems to delineate itself from that of the rest of society, often so sharply that many people believe youth quite naturally obeys a law of its own and has a form of life of its own. During the past decades, male youth organizations have become prominent, especially on German soil. They have, to be sure, the positive value of fellowship. But they also bear a certain hostility to culture, which on occasion becomes evident in isolation, a belligerent attitude toward "the parents," and escape from the female sex.

Continuity with childhood. Unbiased observation will discover no essentially new forces during the period of puberty. All its phenomena can easily be recognized as advanced stages of development that were prepared in childhood. The time of puberty, with its approach to the front of life, its maturation of organs, and its complex of increased physical and psychological sexual demands, faces the expectations of the future as in an experiment. The maturing child now takes up these attitudes toward life and its present and future demands, which are in accordance with its previous training. In the social question and the question of the relationship to one's fellow man, of the I to the thou, comradely, friendly world-philosophical traits will appear—or their opposites, depending on the development of the social feeling during childhood.

In the direction of occupational choice, one notices movements of approach or escape, both varying in degree with the strength of the belief in one's own powers. The evaluation and views of sexuality and the sexual goal of earlier years become very much clearer in the movements of the young man and girl during this stage of greater independence and freedom, and greater tolerance on the part of the adults. All these and other questions of puberty are answered as they were approached long ago, showing the person's social interest developed so far, his striving for significance, and inferiority feelings.

Inadequate maturation. The inadequate preparations from childhood consist mostly in incomplete training for life, be it in the social, occupational, or sexual direction, and in the neglect to develop a self-reliant and self-confident, courageous character. Life in our culture requires schooling and an optimistic, resolved attitude, or else conflicts and contradictions are inescapable, which appear already in childhood, in school, in the family, and in relation to comrades. Their effect is harmful, particularly in dependent individuals, due to their greater sensitivity and indecision, which persistently press toward supposedly less resistance. Thus one frequently finds during puberty, near the front line of life where decisions must be made, secret or open deviations from cultural ways, the meaning of which is plainly directed toward evading a test.

Once one understands the disagreeable fermentations of puberty as attempts at compensation arising from a feeling of weakness, then much of what has been regarded as the phenomenon and effect of puberty resolves itself into the result of a progressive but inadequate maturation. Since children are almost generally inadequately prepared, the test of the puberty period gives rise to conflicts. Youth is almost generally discouraged, the main blame for which rests with the lack of courage of large sections of the population, education for cowardliness, pampering or lack of love, and the burden of all-too-great expectations for the future. Consequently there is widespread inclination to subterfuges, excuses, and evasion of pressing demands.

The frequent attempts to arrange pretenses for a flight from social, occupational, and love problems through an escalation of conflicts deserve special attention. Not from strength, but from weakness, forms of life are then often arrived at that are a mimicry, supposed to create the illusion of strength. Often a senseless fight bursts out in the family; worthless battles against real or imagined authorities attract all available strength; hatred, aversion, and lack of interest for one's occupational activity arise mostly out of fear of defeat; and the normal capacity for love is artificially interfered with through a continuous training in the direction of perversions that seem to guarantee more securely one's own superiority. A tendentiously ignited ego cult represents a disturbing throttling of the social feeling, leads to harmful isolation, and is always connected with oversensitivity and boundless ambition that again and again occasion conflicts and further isolation.

In this critical situation, numerous symptoms appear as signs of a retreating movement, such as compulsion neurosis, hysteria, neurasthenia, anxiety neuroses, and as a picture of complete breakdown, dementia praecox. The path to waywardness and to crime in the more active young people is also an expression of discouragement with regard to the normal role, as is prostitution.

Suicide figures begin to rise during puberty when the tendency toward discouraged but revengeful solutions of conflicts easily gains the upper hand in this kind of individual.

The positive side. Alongside these troublesome puberty phenomena one always finds also heightened values. Further developments are seen in all possible performances and abilities. Independence, reliability, and the feeling of solidarity (*Zusammengehörigkeitsgefühl*) become more prominent. Long-practiced preparations and skills express themselves also as heightened interests, and the permanent acquisition of skills and their further development give the life of the more mature person a more definite direction with regard to activity and vocation. While apparent aptitudes for art and science often disappear during this time, in other cases, the creative ability rises to surprising originality. The forms of life previously gained become more clearly outlined with increasing powers and in their struggle for independence. Guiding ideals, usually still in connection with what has been seen, heard, or read, point to the meaning of the future life that is developing at this point.

4

LOVE AND MARRIAGE

LOVE AS A LIFE TASK[1]

To get to know a person completely, we must understand him also in his love relationships. We must be able to tell whether in matters of love he behaves correctly or incorrectly; and why in one case he may be suited, while in another case he would be unsuited. Quite naturally, the further problem arises: What can we do to prevent errors in love relationships? If we consider that human happiness depends perhaps to the largest part on the solution of the love and marriage problem, we will appreciate that these are most important questions.

One difficulty is brought up by most people right at the start. They say that people are not all alike and that two persons could perhaps have been happier, had each found a different partner. Granted this possibility, this consideration tells us only that the persons in question made a bad choice. But we do not know whether the foundering on the problem of love is due to the erroneous choice, or whether he or she would have foundered on this problem in any case, for deeper reasons. An understanding of the human soul and its moving forces can often spare us from failures.

[1] Original translation of A1926a, pp. 3–9.

The Three Life Tasks

The problem of love relationships is a part of the problem of human life. Its understanding is possible only if we regard the coherence with all other problems of life. Life poses three great task complexes (*Aufgabenkomplexe*), from the solution of which our future, our happiness depend.

Social task. The first life task is the social task in the broadest sense. Life demands of everybody a certain behavior and a very far-reaching ability for contact (*Kontaktfähigkeit*) with our fellow men, a certain behavior within the family, and a formulation of his social attitude. It does matter for the fate of a person what kind of social order he sets as his direction-giving goal, to what extent he thinks in his actions of his own welfare, and to what extent of the welfare of others. His inner choice is often difficult to discern from his outward decisions; often he cannot decide at all in questions of social attitude, and often his viewpoint must be understood in another sense than its outward appearance. This is similar to a person's political attitude. People seldom are satisfied with their political party, and very often one would like to assign them to another party. What counts is always a person's behavior toward the human community, his fellow men in the widest sense, not what he or others think about it.

Occupation. A second life task is that of occupation—that is, the manner in which a person wants to make his abilities serve the general public. The solution of this question illuminates most clearly the essence of a person. For example, when a young man finds every occupation loathsome, we shall provisionally consider him not a suitable fellow man, because either he is not yet sufficiently mature for society, or he may never mature on his own. In most cases by far occupational choice is based on unconscious connections. They are unconscious in that at the time of choice nobody considers that he has taken a step for the benefit of the general public, that he has selected for himself a place in the general division of labor. Of course, what he does in his occupation also counts. One may reach an occupational choice but fail within the occupation, or recognize after a while that one really should have become something else. Frequent change of occupation permits the conclusion that the person in fact would prefer no occupation at all, or perhaps considers himself too good for any occupation–actually, not good enough–and only pretends to go along with it.

Love and Marriage. The third life task that every person must solve is the problem of love and marriage, to which we want to give here our special consideration. The child grows into this problem gradually. His entire surrounding is filled with love and marriage relationships. Unmistakably, the child, already in the very first years of life, attempts to take a stand and to give himself a direction toward this problem. What we hear about this in words is not decisive, because as soon as the child touches upon problems of love an enormous shyness often overcomes him. Some children express quite clearly that they cannot speak about this topic. Others are very devoted to their parents yet are not capable of being affectionate with them. A four-year-old boy returned proffered kisses with slaps in the face because the feeling of an affectionate impulse was uncanny to him, seemed to him frightening–one may even say, humiliating.

Also in looking back on our own lives we notice that every affectionate impulse is accompanied by a sort of sense of shame and the impression that thereby one would become weaker or lose in value. This is very remarkable and requires an explanation. Our culture being generally orientated toward a masculine ideal, we grow up in the frame of mind that an affectionate impulse is a disgrace. Accordingly, in school, literature, and any environment, the children are continuously trained to see in love a kind of unmanliness. Sometimes they express this quite clearly, and some go so far that one may say they evade emotion.

The Logic of Social Living

The child's first impulses of affection appear very early. As they develop, one can very easily note that they are all impulses of the social feeling. This is evidently innate, since it appears quite regularly. From the degree of its development we can appraise an individual's attitude to life.

The very concept of "human being" includes our entire understanding of social feeling. We cannot imagine that a human being could be designated as such after having lost it. Likewise, throughout history we find no human beings living in isolation. They always lived in groups, unless separated from one another artificially or through insanity. Darwin showed that animals with a less favorable position with regard to nature live in groups. Their vitality becomes effective by forming groups, unconsciously following a principle of self-preservation. Those that lived singly, in whose stepmotherly development social feeling was lacking, perished, victims of natural selection. The principle of natural selection is also dangerous for man, since, in facing nature, his physical equipment is most stepmotherly of all.

The situation of the inferiority and inadequacy of the human race develops in the whole race and in the individual a continuous drive and coercion that drive us on, until an approximate condition of rest is reached and some form of existence appears assured.

We are still on this path, and today it is perhaps the best consolation for man to realize that our present situation is only a point of transition, a momentary phase of human development. He will naturally best pass through this phase, in reference to all problems of life, who is in accord with the actual conditions and does justice to the logic of the facts, whereas those who resist this logic, naturally will meet a merciless destiny. In the deepest sense, the feeling for the logic of human living together is social feeling.

The entire development of the child demands his embeddedness in a situation in which social feeling is present. His life and health are assured only if there are persons at hand who take his part. A newly born calf, for example, can very soon discriminate poisonous plants from others. The newly born human, however, due to the inferiority of his organism, depends on the social feeling of the adult. The child must for a long time be taken care of, taught, and trained until he can look after himself.

When we consider the abilities of which we are particularly proud, which assure us priority above other creatures–such as reason, logic, language, our understanding and preference for everything that is beautiful and good–we can see that the single human being could never have produced them. They are, so to speak, born only of the group mind (*Massenseele*). Thereby further needs have arisen that never could have burdened the single individual–and are satisfied. For a single human being, without coherence with a community, conscious, deliberate logic would be totally indifferent. He would not need to talk, it would not matter whether he were good or bad. Without a relationship to a human community or to a fellow man, these concepts would lose all meaning, as in the case of single animals. All human qualities, all achievements of the human mind, are conceivable only in the coherence (*Zusammenhang*) of men among each other.

Love, Part of Social Feeling

The coherence of men among each other is necessitated not only by the pressing needs of the day, but also by our sexual organization. The division of humanity into two sexes, far from creating a separation, means an eternal compulsion toward one another. It creates the feeling of being mutually related, because in the veins of each a common blood flows, because each one is flesh from the flesh of another.

The marriage laws of the various peoples can be understood only from the viewpoint of love as a common bond of the entire group. Marriage and sexual relations among members of the same family were interdicted because this would have led to an isolation of the families. Poetry, religions, the holy commandments are directed against incest and intended to eradicate it. While scholars have puzzled over the reason for the natural aversion of family members toward one another, we understand it quite easily on the basis of the social feeling that develops in each child and that eliminates all possibilities that could lead to an isolation of man.

Now we can understand that love in its essential meaning, the relationship of the sexes, is always connected with social feeling and cannot be separated from it. Love, as a relationship of two, has, as a part of social feeling, its own laws and is a necessary component of the preservation of human society. One cannot think of a community without it. He who affirms the community necessarily also affirms love. He who has community feeling must favor marriage or a form of love of equal or higher value. On the other hand, a person whose social feeling is throttled, who has not arrived at a free development of his nature within humanity, will also show a strange form of love relationships.

Now we can draw a few conclusions that will facilitate an overview of this large area of love relationships and suddenly shed some light on it. A person whose social development is impaired, who has no friends, has not become a real fellow man, whose world view contradicts social feeling, and who perhaps has also not solved his occupational problem well—that is, one who is more or less completely lost to the community, is bound to have difficulties in his love relationships. Such persons will hardly be in a position to solve the erotic problem. They will take strange ways, will create difficulties, and will, where they actually find difficulties, reach for them as for a safeguarding excuse.

DISTURBANCES OF LOVE RELATIONSHIPS[2]

Let us consider more closely the difficulties people create in their love relationships, and thereby gain a deeper insight into

[2] Original translation of A1926a, pp. 9–18, with some paragraphs rearranged.

the entire problem. In a person's love relationships his entire personality is involved. We can understand his personality from his love relationships, as well as guess at his particular sexual aspirations from an understanding of his personality as a whole.[3]

Seeking Power over the Partner

Obligating through love. Most frequently we find within the sexual relationship the erroneous assumption that love is an obligation for the other party. When we look around, and also observe ourselves, we will see that very often we commit the error of believing that the beloved person, by the mere fact of being loved, is obligated to us. This error seems somehow to be contained in our entire form of looking at things (*Anschauungsform*). It originates in childhood and the relationships with the family, where indeed the love of one is almost equal to the obligation of the other. In the adult, it is a remnant from childhood. The resulting excesses center around the thought: "Because I love you, you must do such and such." Thereby a much more severe tone is often introduced in the relationships of persons who are really devoted to each other. The need for power of the one who, on the strength of his own love, wants to draw the other into his schema, demands that the other's steps, expressions, achievements, etc., take place according to his wishes, "because he loves this person." This can easily turn into tyranny. A trace of this is found perhaps in every love relationship.

Thus we see the same factor permeating human love life that also otherwise leads always to disturbances of fellowship: the striving for power and personal superiority.

In a human community, one must respect the freedom of the personal individuality to the extent of leaving the other

[3] In the year in which this essay was published, Adler introduced the term "life style" into his writings. Thus we find here still the terms "entire personality," "personality," and "personality as a whole," which Adler subsequently equated with life style, while a few pages below he actually uses the term "life style" (p. 113).

person free choices. He who strives for personal superiority prevents his connection with a community. He does not want to fit into the whole, but wants the subordination of the others. Thereby he naturally disturbs the harmony in life, in society, among his fellow men. Since by nature no one wants permanently to have a yoke placed on him, those persons who, even in their love relationships are striving for power over the other, must meet with oversized difficulties. If they continue their inclination for presumption and superiority into their sex lives, they must seek a partner who appears to submit, or struggle with one who seeks superiority or victory on his own or in response to the situation. In the case of submission, love is transformed into slavery; in the second case, there will be a continuous, mutually destructive power struggle by which no harmony will ever be reached.

Selecting a subordinate partner. The ways of doing so vary greatly. Some domineering persons tremble so much for their ambition, their power, that they look only for a partner in whom there is no danger of superiority, who always appears to subordinate himself. These are by no means always worthless persons with high ambition. To be possessed by this striving for power is in our culture a generally prevalent trait causing immeasurable harm to the development of humanity.

In this light we can understand the relatively frequent strange phenomenon that people will in their love choice descend into a much lower and unsuitable social milieu. For example, a study of Goethe's love life would show that this ambitious man was extremely insecure in his love affairs. Concerned with the highest problem of humanity, he surprised his fellow men (*Mitwelt*) by marrying his cook. Emphasizing the equal worth of men, as we do, we are of course not indignant about this. But we regard such action as out of keeping and want to understand it from that individual's viewpoint by examining his ultimate intention.

By our norm those persons will find each other who are socially and by their education and preparation for life best suited for each other. Suitors whose choices deviate from the general expectation are mostly persons who face the love problem with extreme hesitation and prejudices, are afraid of their sexual partner and, therefore, are looking for a partner in whom they suspect less power and strength. It is of course possible that someone may deviate from the norm through a feeling of strength. But mostly it is done through weakness.

Such a choice appears to some of these careful individuals as an extremely happy solution, not understanding that their ultimate intention is to conceal their deeper motives through love and sexuality, and convinced that only Cupid is involved here. But as a rule such a relationship turns out poorly and has many disadvantages–not that the intellectually or socially "superior" partner would be disappointed, or that difficulties of a social nature would occur when the "inferior" partner would not satisfy certain requirements of family and social life. These and other external factors could be eliminated and bridged, if the ultimate intention of the "superior" partner could be realized. But strangely it is the "inferior" partner who does not tolerate for long seeing his weakness abused. Even if he does not understand what goes on, he nevertheless cannot get rid of the feeling that his shortcomings are being abused. From this feeling he takes to a kind of revenge; he will try to show that he is not less than the other.

There are many conspicuous cases of this kind. Often a young, cultured, outstandingly intelligent girl throws herself into the arms of an insignificant, often even immoral person, perhaps sometimes with the idea of saving a man whom she appears to love from the clutches of alcoholism, gambling, or indolence. Never yet have such people been saved through love. This action fails almost regularly. The "inferior" partner feels under all circumstances oppressed by his inferior classification. He does not let himself be loved and be saved, because the moving forces of his attitude to life are quite different and not recognizable by ordinary intelligence, the "common sense."[4] He has perhaps long ago given up hope ever to amount to anything and sees in every situation that makes on him requirements as a fellow man a new danger that his presumed inferiority could become clearly apparent.

Many persons also are interested only in physically

[4] The English phrase "common sense" is used in the German original.

deficient or much older love partners. These cases rightfully attract our attention and call for an explanation. Sometimes we find a natural explanation arising from a particular situation. But even then this inclination always corresponds to a life style of taking the line of least resistance.

Predatory desire. Other persons fall in love almost only with partners who are already engaged. This strange fact may reveal various intentions. It may mean, "No," regarding the demands of love, striving for the impossible, or an unfulfillable ideal. But it may also mean, "wanting to take something away from another," a trait carried over into sexuality from the life style.

The biographies of famous persons show that in our complex culture people grow up with an extraordinary eagerness to rob, to take away. The longing for a married woman always results in further actions—namely, to seize the love object—although this is often disguised in the most noble form. Richard Wagner was apparently of this kind. Almost all his poetic creations contain the meaning, the complication, that the hero desires a woman who already belongs to another. Wagner's own life also shows this characteristic.[5]

Evading Marriage

Many people are not quite sufficiently mature for society, see in love and marriage relationships a danger zone, and express their immature views in various ways that are, on the surface, often unintelligible. Regarding these questions, which continuously bother them, they speak in generalities that, in some context, could be true and would not necessarily be a deception. For example, when somebody who is also otherwise timid believes he does not marry "because life these days is so difficult," each word is true enough. But it is also true for those who do marry. Such truths are expressed only by those who would have said "No" even without these truths. In that event they would have reached for another "truth." It

[5] This paragraph has been moved from p. 16 of the original.

would be undiplomatic to support a preconceived intention with a bad argument when good ones are available everywhere. Alarmingly, many people try to escape from the solution of the life problems, and this also takes the guise of sex.

Unrequited love. This is the case in most instances of repeatedly unrequited love. It is a means for realizing, with a pretense of justification, the life goal of turning away from life, from the world. In such cases an unhappy love cannot be unhappy enough to fulfill its purpose. It strikes persons with a readiness to run away from the problems of life, especially those of love, which sometimes receives welcome reinforcement by a trick, a device. This is not always completely invented but is attached to some actual life relationship. Then it does not look like a device but resembles the obvious result of an experience.

We can also "make" a person unattainable. Often the suitor has, from the start, the impression that he will not be received well, but makes this an occasion for greater action. He believes he cannot live without the beloved person and courts her, although any objective observer would consider it improbable that his love would ever be requited. He even says so to himself. Often such courting takes a form apt to provoke resistance—for example, by being extremely vehement, or occurring at a time before any guarantees for living together are given. Such courtships are aimed at unrequited love. A surprisingly large number of persons steer toward this goal.

Some people have been infatuated even without knowing whether that person exists. This clearly expresses their ultimate intention not to have anything to do with love and marriage. Their infatuation can in all probability never be realized.

One should think, from the outside, that such behavior was not part of human nature. But such a person is an "escapist" throughout, and unrequited love provides him with an excellent hiding place. When he carries his unrequited love with him for five or ten years, he is during this entire time safe from all other solutions of this problem. Of course, he has suffered, paid the expenses for the realization of his intention.

But his goal—which has remained unconscious to himself, which he himself did not understand—to stay away from the solution of the love and marriage problem, has thereby been reached with a good conscience and justification. Such a goal and solution are not compatible with the conditions of this earth and the logic of human living together. They are actually the deepest tragedy rather than a solution. Only by this ultimate deepest insight is corrective intervention possible.

High ideals. For the escapist, one frequently tested device is especially recommended. Let him create a new idea, a special ideal. Let him measure by this ideal all persons who cross his path in life. The consequence is that no one will prove suitable; they all deviate from the ideal. When he refuses and eliminates them, his action looks reasonable and well founded. But when we examine an individual case, we find that such a reasonably choosing person, even without his ideal, is willing from the start to say "No." The ideal contains desirable goals of frankness, honesty, courage, etc. But these concepts can be extended and stretched at will until they exceed any human measure. Thus we have at our disposal the love of something that we have previously "made" unattainable.

This device has various possibilities of concretization. We can love a person who was present once for a short time, made an impression, disappeared, and can now no longer be found. One would have to look all over the world to find him. At first we are touched by such fond and faithful love. However, the condition for the realization of such love on earth is superhuman and raises our suspicion.[6]

Fear and Lack of Reserve

Generally, the feeling of insecurity determines many forms of sexuality. There are young men who like only older women [as mentioned earlier], somehow in the erroneous

[6] These two paragraphs have been moved here from pp. 14–15 of the original.

opinion that in this case living together would be less difficult. They disclose their feelings of weakness also through a certain need for motherly care. They are usually pampered persons who very much want to lean on somebody, who "still need a nursemaid." They can never have enough safeguards against the other sex, and become extremely disquieted when facing it.

There are in our culture alarmingly many such insecure persons with a strong blemish of our phase of development—the fear of love and marriage. It is a general trait of the times. Our society is full of escapists. Through some unhappy and erroneous attitude, they are always as if in flight, always chased and persecuted. Some men isolate themselves and hide. Some girls don't even dare to go on the street, convinced that all men are courting them and that they would always be only the object of attacks. This is pure vanity, capable of completely spoiling the life of a person.

Experiences and knowledge can be put to good use and to bad use. Among the bad uses is the exaggerated reversal of an error, which is equally an error. The opposite of keeping back and being taciturn is openness, and thus we find people who make errors by being open. They always offer themselves to others. Although it is very nice openly to confess one's love, we are firmly convinced that in our complex culture this is a serious mistake. The reason is that there is nobody who could simply tolerate this offer, and the one who made it so hastily will not only have to bear the pain of regret and the burden of resulting inhibitions, but will also disturb the partner in the spontaneous development of his love impulses. Because of the generally prevailing abuse of love and the existing tension and struggle between the sexes, the partner will never be quite sure whether the offer was genuine and true, or whether perhaps bad intentions were hidden behind it. There are no fixed rules—we must take the particularity of the partner into account and go by the given conditions of our culture. Today it appears rather advisable to hold back one's inclinations somewhat.

THE SPECIAL SITUATION OF THE ARTIST[7]

Love plays a special part in the lives of artists—happy love as well as, more often, unhappy love. Unrequited love is today so general that almost everybody has at one time become the victim of it and its hardships. Among persons who face life with particular sensitivity, the artist plays a prominent role. He stands out by the very fact that he seeks in his art a life "aside from life," does not work in actual reality, but seeks a substitute world (*Ersatzwelt*), and is almost repulsed by reality. However, he becomes an artist only when he forms his creations so that they advance the real world. A creation becomes a work of art only by having the most general value, in that the artist found in it the way back to reality and the community.

In deviating from real life, one is inclined to experience the institution of love and marriage, with its emphasis on the reality of life as hostile and disturbing. Many artists take the ties of life literally as ties, shackles, or obstacles. They even develop them in their fantasy beyond bounds. Once they sense them as boundless obstacles, they can hardly overcome them. They find themselves in their love relationships before an insoluble task, and herein show not only the movements of a lover, but at the same time and to a much stronger degree the movements of a person fleeing from love. This is expressed in their thoughts and creations, which mirror the human problems in intensified form. The partner of the other sex is felt as somehow overpowering, and soon the field of love assumes the character of a danger.

This thought is found almost literally in communications from poets and writers. All problematical people have this tendency because they are all extremely ambitious and sensitive and take any impairment of their power as a serious insult or danger.

Art is today a predominantly masculine art. It contains the

[7] Original translation of A1926a, pp. 18–21.

masculine tradition, presents predominantly masculine problems, and raises the female to a magic or frightening figure, which she is in the eyes of many men. Women cannot keep step with this masculine ideal of the times. They find the practice of art difficult not because they would not be capable, but because they cannot serve the exaggerated masculine ideal.

Regarding the female as danger, the poet Baudelaire[8] says: "I have never been able to think of a beautiful woman without having, at the same time, the sense of an immense danger."

A person who has entered this presumed "danger zone" will display a sequence of defensive and safeguarding movements. Hebbel,[9] as a youth, in a letter to his friend, describes his feelings approximately as follows: "Of course, I live here again opposite the most beautiful girl in town and am over my ears in love. But I hope that here too the antidote will soon be found alongside the poison. . . . And if today I should still see her lover climbing through her window, I would be through with her." From the first sentence we would really have expected a different ending.

The female as danger is an enduring guiding ideal in art; for example, the paintings of Rops[10] represent the female as danger, terror, or at least as an enormous power. In the Preface to *A Thousand and One Nights* the author, particularly frightened, points to the cunning and slyness of a woman who, through incredible inventiveness, saved her life from a man.

Also one of the oldest forms of art, the Bible, whose particular mood grips everybody from earliest childhood on, is permeated by the constant thought that the female represents danger. Thus a child will grow up in shyness, imbalance, and timidity toward the female. Also, Homer's *Iliad* paints with great precision the misfortune caused by a woman. In all works of poetry, in all works of art resounds the problem of

[8] Charles Baudelaire (1821–67), French lyrical poet.
[9] Friedrich Hebbel (1813–63), German poet and dramatist.
[10] Félicien Rops (1833–98), Belgian painter and etcher.

the day: woman the danger. Grillparzer[11] says of himself: "I have rescued myself from love into art."

How unrequited love will work itself out in a given person depends on his total attitude toward life, his life line.[12] If in the face of difficulties one loses his courage and calls off his activity, foundering in love may mean foundering in life. But this is then not a consequence of unrequited love itself. One who goes by the plan of being stimulated by difficulties will pull himself together after unrequited love and arrive at great achievements. A courageous person will draw a different conclusion than a defeated person. Popular psychology frequently points to the great achievements after unrequited love and sometimes recommends it like a medicine. But we know of people who have achieved great things without unrequited love. The kernel of truth is that artists are particularly seized and captivated by the problem of love.

The life of Goethe is, in this respect, particularly informative. He always saw danger in the female and always took flight before her and love. The guiding line of Faust is an eternal seeking for a solution of the love problem. With his own tensions, impulses, and strivings, Goethe built his world, dissatisfied with the facts of life, and conjured generally human concerns before our eyes. It is the greatness of his art that all strings in us resonate when he sounds the eternally new song of the tension between the sexes. Entangled in this tension, men fear that devotion is synonymous with loss of personality, with bondage or slavery.

Here Schleiermacher[13] is also to be mentioned who, in a wonderful essay, tries to prove that love is not such a simple matter, and that it would be foolish to believe that when a man entered adulthood he already knew something about love. Actually, everyone should go through a certain preparation, a preparatory school of an easier sort. This pure idealist,

[11] Franz Grillparzer (1791–1872), Austrian dramatist.

[12] Life line and guiding line are further earlier equivalents of life style.

[13] Friedrich Schleiermacher (1768–1834), German theologian and philosopher.

who is greatly venerated by the most religious people, is also convinced that in love, men do not find one another easily.

MEETING DIFFICULTIES[14]

In my lectures "Understanding Human Nature," which are regularly attended by about five hundred persons, the questions directed to me are largely on love–a sign that people find their way less easily in this question than perhaps that of occupation.[15]

Why are there so few happy love relationships? Because we are still not the real human beings, not yet mature for love, in arrears with being fellow men. We fight against it with all our means because we are afraid. Think of the opposition to coeducation, which only wants the sexes early in life to lose their shyness and fear, and have an opportunity to know each other better.

There is no fixed rule for meeting difficulties in love relationships. The peculiarity of a person's eroticism is a flourish of his total personality, which must be comprehended in each single case. To change a person's erroneous eroticism we must comprehend all his expressions in their coherence, and change his personality and its relationships to the surrounding world. A person's line of movement, which will assert itself also in love, may force him to seek an unrequited love and to persist in it, or it may let him take such an experience more lightly and lead him upward. If a person saturated with personal ambition cannot bear any kind of denial, it may suggest suicide. This is an error, which can be explained from the total context. In our society, which demands subordination, it will offer the opportunity for a highly tragic situation–connecting with the escape from life revenge against society and individual persons.

[14] Original translation of A1926a, pp. 21–23.

[15] Adler refers here to the popular lecture series he gave for several years at the Volksheim, Vienna's most important adult education institute at the time (Furtmüller, 1964, p. 374). These lectures, subsequently published under the same title, became the most widely read and translated book of Adler (A1927a).

Love is cultivated and love relationships become beautified and refined through the cultivation and development of the all-encompassing social feeling. Love relationships are not formed suddenly but show a long preparation. The erotic tie is always present among human beings, but certain requirements must be met to make it felt and visible as love.

The beginning of love impulses goes back to those distant childhood days when they were not yet erotic, not yet sexually tinged—the days when the broad stream of social feeling still took the form of attachment and affection. Only that general human relationship was visible that, as between mother and child, connects human beings immediately. The enduring tie between single individuals that serves eternity and the preservation of humanity, which we call love, was not yet formed. It is a tie and perpetuation at the same time. One cannot shape these relationships at will, but rather must permit them to develop.

Knowledge of these matters has not yet matured because man is capable of self-deception regarding the processes of his own soul. Both sexes are easily caught in the whirlpool of prestige politics (*Prestigepolitik*). Then they are forced to play a role with which neither can cope, which leads to disturbing the harmlessness and spontaneity of their lives, and saturates them with prejudices against which every trace of true joy and happiness must of course disappear.[16]

A person who has absorbed these thoughts will naturally not move on earth free from mistakes, but he will at least remain aware of the right way and be able, instead of increasing his errors, steadily to diminish them.

UNDERSTANDING THE TASK OF MARRIAGE[17]

In a certain district of Germany there is an old custom for testing whether an engaged couple are suited for married life

[16] This paragraph is very similar to one on p. 25.

[17] Reprinted from A1931b, pp. 263–68. In accordance with today's usage, in all sections reprinted from A1931b (that is, the rest of this chapter), "mankind" has been replaced by "humanity."

together. Before the wedding ceremony, the bride and bridegroom are brought to a clearing, where a tree trunk has been cut down. Here they are given a two-handed saw and set to work to saw the trunk across. This is a test of how far they are willing to co-operate with each other. It is a task for two people. If there is no trust between them, they will tug against each other and accomplish nothing. If one of them wishes to take the lead and do everything by himself, then, even if the other gives way, the task will take twice as long. They must both have initiative, but their initiatives must combine together. These German villagers have recognized that co-operation is the chief prerequisite for marriage.

Co-operation for the General Welfare

If I were asked to say what love and marriage mean, I should give the following definition, incomplete as it may be:

"Love, with its fulfillment, marriage, is the most intimate devotion toward a partner of the other sex, expressed in physical attraction, in comradeship, and in the decision to have children. It can easily be shown that love and marriage are one side of co-operation–not a co-operation for the welfare of two persons only, but a co-operation also for the welfare of humanity."

This standpoint, that love and marriage are a co-operation for the welfare of humanity, throws light on every aspect of the problem. Even physical attraction, the most important of all human strivings, has been a most necessary development for humanity. As I have explained so often, humanity, suffering from imperfect organs, has been none too well equipped for life on the crust of this poor planet, earth. The chief way to preserve human life was to propagate it; hence our fertility and the continual striving of physical attraction.

In our own days, we find difficulties and dissensions arising over all the problems of love. Married couples are confronted with these difficulties, parents are concerned with them, the whole of society is involved in them. If we are trying, therefore, to come to a right conclusion, our approach must be quite without prejudice. We must forget what we have learned and try to investigate, as far as we can, without letting other considerations interfere with a full and free discussion.

I do not mean that we can judge the problem of love and marriage as if it were an entirely isolated problem. A human being can never be wholly free in this way: He can never reach solutions for his problems purely along the line of his private ideas. Every human being is bound by definite ties; his development takes place within a definite framework, and he must conform his decisions to this framework. These three main ties are set by the facts that we are living in one particular place in the universe and must develop with the limits and possibilities that our circumstances set us; that we are living among others of our own kind to whom we must learn to adapt ourselves; and that we are living in two sexes, with the future of our race dependent on the relations of these two sexes.

If an individual is interested in his fellows and in the welfare of humanity, everything he does will be guided by the interests of his fellows. He will try to solve the problem of love and marriage as if the welfare of others were involved. He does not need to know that he is trying to solve it in this way. If you ask him, he will perhaps be unable to give a scientific account of his aims. But he will spontaneously seek the welfare and improvement of humanity, and this interest will be visible in all his activities.

There are other human beings who are not so much concerned with the welfare of humanity. Instead of taking as their underlying view of life "What can I contribute to my fellows?" "How can I fit in as part of the whole?" they ask rather, "What is the use of life?" "What can I get out of it?" "What does it pay?" "Are other people considering me enough?" "Am I properly appreciated?" If this attitude is behind an individual's approach to life, he will try to solve the problem of love and marriage in the same way. He will ask always: "What can I get out of it?"

Love is not a purely natural task, as some psychologists believe. Sex is a drive or instinct; but the question of love and marriage is not quite simply how we are to satisfy this drive. Wherever we look, we find that our drives and instincts are developed, cultivated, refined. We have repressed some of our desires and inclinations. On behalf of our fellow beings, we have learned how not to annoy each other. We have learned how to dress ourselves and how to be clean. Even our hunger does not have a merely natural outlet; we have cultivated tastes and manners in eating. Our drives have all been adapted to our common culture; they all reflect the efforts we have learned to make for the welfare of humanity and for our life in association.

If we apply this understanding to the problem of love and marriage, we shall see, here again, that the interest of the whole, the interest in humanity, must always be involved. This interest is primary. There is no advantage in discussing any of the aspects of love and marriage, in proposing reliefs, changes, new regulations, or new institutions, before we have seen that the problem can be solved only in its whole coherence, only by considering human welfare as a whole. Perhaps we shall improve; perhaps we shall find more complete answers to the problem. If we do, they will be better answers because they take fuller account of the fact that we are living in two sexes, on the crust of this earth, where association is necessary. Insofar as our answers already take account of these conditions, the truth in them can stand forever.

Task for Two Equal Partners

When we use this approach, our first finding in the love problem is that it is a task for two individuals. For many people this is bound to be a new task. To some degree we have been educated to work alone; to some degree, to work in a team or a group. We have generally had little experience of working two by two. These new conditions, therefore, raise a difficulty; but it is a difficulty easier to solve if these two people have been interested in their fellows, for then they can learn more easily to be interested in each other.

We could even say that for a full solution of this co-operation of two, each partner must be more interested in the other than in himself. This is the only basis on which love and marriage can be successful. We shall already be able to see in what way many opinions of marriage and many proposals for its reform are mistaken.

If each partner is to be more interested in the other partner than in himself, there must be equality. If there is to be so intimate a devotion, neither partner can feel subdued nor overshadowed. Equality is only possible if both partners have this attitude. It should be the effort of each to ease and enrich the life of the other. In this way each is safe. Each feels that he is worthwhile; each feels that he is needed.

Here we find the fundamental guarantee of marriage, the fundamental meaning of happiness in this relation. It is the feeling that you are worthwhile, that you cannot be replaced, that your partner needs you, that you are acting well, that you are a fellow man and a true friend.

It is not possible for a partner in a co-operative task to accept a position of subservience. Two people cannot live together fruitfully if one wishes to rule and force the other to obey. In our present conditions many men and, indeed, many women are convinced that it is the man's part to rule and dictate, to play the leading role, to be the master. This is the reason why we have so many unhappy marriages. Nobody can bear a position of inferiority without anger and disgust.

Comrades must be equal, and when people are equal, they will always find a way to settle their difficulties. They will agree, for example, in questions of having children. They know that a decision for sterility involves their own part in giving a pledge for the future of humanity. They will agree in questions of education; and they will be stimulated to solve their problems as they occur, because they know that the children of unhappy marriages are penalized and cannot develop well.

In our present-day civilization people are not often well prepared for co-operation. Our training has been too much toward individual success, toward considering what we can get out of life rather than what we can give to it. It will be easily understood that where we get two people living together in the intimate way that marriage demands, any failure in co-operation, in the ability to be interested in somebody else, will have the gravest results. Most people are experiencing this close relationship for the first time. They are unaccustomed to consulting another human being's interests and aims, desires, hopes, and ambitions. They are not prepared for the problems of a common task. We need not be surprised at the many mistakes we see around us; but we can examine the facts and learn how to avoid mistakes in the future.

EDUCATION AND TRAINING[18]

No crisis of adult life is met without previous training. We always respond in conformity with our style of living. The preparation for marriage is not overnight. In a child's characteristic behavior, in his attitudes, thoughts, and actions, we can see how he is training himself for adult situations. In its main features his approach to love is already established by the fifth or sixth year.

Early Sex Education

Early in the development of a child we can see that he is already forming his outlook on love and marriage. We should not imagine that he is showing sexual promptings in our adult sense of the term. He is making up his mind about one aspect of the general social life of which he feels himself a part. Love and marriage are factors of his environment: They enter into his conception of his own future. He must have some comprehension of them, take up some stand about these problems.

When children give such early evidence of their interest in the other sex and choose for themselves the partners whom they like, we should never interpret it as a mistake, or a nuisance, or a precocious sex influence. Still less should we

[18] Reprinted from A1931b, pp. 268–72.

deride it or make a joke of it. We should take it as a step forward in their preparation for love and marriage. Instead of making a trifle out of it, we should rather agree with the child that love is a marvelous task, a task for which he should be prepared, a task on behalf of the whole of humanity. Thus we can implant an ideal in the child's mind, and later in life children will be able to meet each other as very well-prepared comrades and as friends in an intimate devotion. It is revealing to observe that children are spontaneous and wholehearted adherents of monogamy—and this often in spite of the fact that the marriages of their parents are not always harmonious and happy.

I should never encourage parents to explain the physical relations of sex too early in life or to explain more than their children wish to learn. You can understand that the way in which a child looks on the problems of marriage is of the greatest importance. If he is taught in a mistaken way, he can see them as a danger or as something altogether beyond him. In my own experience children who were introduced to the facts of adult relations in early life—at four, five or six years of age, and children who had precocious experiences—are always more scared of love in later life. Bodily attraction suggests to them also the idea of danger. If a child is more grown-up when he has his first explanations and experiences, he is not nearly so frightened: There is so much less opportunity for him to make mistakes in understanding the right relations. The key to helpfulness is never to lie to a child, never to evade his questions, to understand what is behind his questions, to explain only as much as we are sure he can understand. Officious and intrusive information can cause great harm.

In this problem of life, as in all others, it is better for a child to be independent and learn what he wants to know by his own efforts. If there is trust between himself and his parents, he can suffer no injury. He will always ask what he needs to know. There is a common superstition that children can be misled by the explanations of their comrades. I have never seen a child, otherwise healthy, who suffered harm in this way. Children do not swallow everything that their schoolmates tell them; for the most part children are very critical, and, if they are not certain that what they have been told is true, they will ask their parents or their brothers and sisters. I must confess, too, that I have often found children more delicate and tactful in these affairs than their elders.

Impressions from Immediate Surroundings

Even the physical attraction of adult life is already being trained in childhood. The impressions the child gains with regard to sympathy and attraction, the impressions given by the members of the other sex in his immediate surroundings —these are the beginnings of physical attraction. When a boy gains these impressions from his mother, his sisters, or the girls around him, his selection of physically attractive types in later life will be influenced by their similarity to these members of his earlier environment. Sometimes he is influenced also by the creations of art: Everybody is drawn in this way by an ideal of personal beauty. Thus in later life the individual has no longer a *free choice* in the broadest sense but a choice only along the lines of his training.

This search for beauty is not a meaningless search. Our aesthetic emotions are always based on a feeling for health and for the improvement and future of humanity; the symbols of the way in which we wish our children to develop. This is the beauty that is always drawing us.

Sometimes if a boy experiences difficulties with his mother, and a girl with her father (as happens often if the co-operation in marriage is not firm), they look for an antithetic type. If, for example, the boy's mother has nagged him and bullied him, if he is weak and afraid of being dominated, he may find sexually attractive only those women who appear not to be dominating. It is easy for him to make mistakes: He can look for a partner whom he can subdue, and a happy marriage is never possible without equality. Sometimes, if he wants to prove himself powerful and strong, he looks for a partner who also seems to be strong, either because he prefers strength or because he finds in her more of a challenge to prove his own strength.

If his disagreement with his mother is very great, his preparation for love and marriage may be hindered, and even physical attraction to the other sex may be blocked. There are many degrees of this obstruction; where it is complete, he will exclude the other sex entirely and become perverted.

We are always better prepared if the marriage of our parents has been harmonious. Children gain their earliest impressions of what marriage is like from the life of their parents, and it is not astonishing that the greatest number of failures in life are among the children of broken marriages and unhappy family life. If the parents are not able themselves to co-operate, it will be impossible for them to teach co-operation to their children.

We can often best consider the fitness of an individual for marriage by learning whether he was trained in the right kind of family life and by observing his attitude toward his parents, sisters, and brothers. The important factor is where he gained his preparation for love and marriage.

We must be careful on this point, however. We know that a man is not determined by his environment but by the estimate he makes of his environment. His estimate can be useful. It is possible that he had very unhappy experiences of family life in his parents' home, but this may only stimulate him to do better in his own family life. He may be striving to prepare himself well for marriage. We must never judge or exclude a human being because he has an unfortunate family life behind him.

PROPER AND IMPROPER PREPARATION[19]

The worst preparation is when an individual is always looking for his own interest. If he has been trained in this way he will be thinking all the while what pleasure or excitement he can get out of life. He will always be demanding freedom and re-

[19] Reprinted from A1931b, pp. 272–78.

liefs, never considering how he can ease and enrich the life of his partner. This is a disastrous approach. I should compare him to a man who tries to put a horse's collar on from the tail end. It is not a sin, but it is a mistaken method.

Proper and Improper Concepts of Marriage

In preparing our attitude to love, therefore, we should not always be looking for mitigations and ways of avoiding responsibility. The comradeship of love could not be firm if there were hesitation and doubt. Co-operation demands a decision for eternity; and we only regard those unions as real examples of love and real marriages in which a fixed and unalterable decision has been taken. In this decision we include the decision to have children, to educate them and train them in co-operation, and to make them, as far as we can, real fellow men, real equal and responsible members of the human race.

A good marriage is the best means we have for bringing up the future generation of humanity; and marriage should always have this in view. Marriage is really a task; it has its own rules and laws; we cannot select one part and evade the others without infringing the eternal law of this earth crust, co-operation.

It is impossible to have the real intimate devotion of love if we limit our responsibility to five years or regard the marriage as a trial period.[20] If men or women contemplate such an escape, they do not collect all their powers for the task. In none of the serious and important tasks of life do we arrange such a "getaway." We cannot love and be limited.

All those very well-meaning and good-hearted people who are trying to find a relief for marriage are on the wrong path. The reliefs they propose would damage and restrict the efforts of couples who were entering marriage; they would make it

[20] This is an allusion to the writings of Judge Benjamin Lindsey (1927), who proposed a companionate marriage which, in many ways similar to earlier ideas of trial marriage, was widely discussed in the late 1920s and early 1930s.

easier for them to find a way out and to omit the work they should do in the task on which they have decided. I know that there are many difficulties in our social life and that they hinder many people from solving the problem of love and marriage in the right way, even though they would like to solve it. It is not love and marriage, however, that I want to sacrifice; I want to sacrifice the difficulties of our social life.

We know what characteristics are necessary for a love partnership—to be faithful and true and trustworthy, not to be reserved, not to be self-seeking. . . . If a person believes that unfaithfulness is all in the day's work, he is not properly prepared for marriage. It is not even possible to carry through a true comradeship if both partners have agreed to preserve their freedom. This is not comradeship. In comradeship we are not free in every direction. We have bound ourselves to our co-operation.

A Case Example

Let me give an example of how such a private agreement, not adapted to the success of the marriage or the welfare of humanity, can harm both partners. I remember a case where a divorced man and a divorced woman married. They were cultivated and intelligent people and hoped very much that their new venture in marriage would be better than the last. They did not know, however, how their first marriages had come to ruin; they were looking for a right way without having seen their lack of social interest. They professed themselves free-thinkers, and they wished to have an easy marriage in which they would never run the risk of being bored by each other. They proposed, therefore, that each of them should be perfectly free in every direction; they should do whatever they wanted to do, but they should trust each other enough to tell everything that happened. On this point the husband seemed to be more courageous. Whenever he came home he had many adventures to tell his wife, and she seemed to enjoy them vastly and to be very proud of her husband's successes. She was always intending to begin a flirtation or a love relation herself; but before she had taken the first step, she began to suffer from agoraphobia. She could no longer go out alone; her neurosis kept her to her room; if she took a step beyond the door she was so scared that she was compelled to return. This agoraphobia was a protection against the decision she had made; but there was more to it than this. At last, since she was unable to go out alone, her husband was compelled to stay by her side. You see how the logic of marriage broke through their decision. The husband could no longer be a free-thinker because he must remain with his wife. She herself could make no use of her freedom because she was afraid to go out alone. If this woman were cured, she would be forced to reach a better understanding of marriage, and the husband, too, would have to regard it as a co-operative task.

Various Improper Preparations

Other mistakes are made at the very beginning of the marriage. A child who has been pampered at home often feels neglected in marriage. He has not been trained to adapt himself to social life. A pampered child may develop into a great tyrant in marriage; the other partner feels victimized, feels himself in a cage, and begins to resist. It is interesting to observe what happens when two pampered children marry each other. Each of them is claiming interest and attention, and neither can be satisfied. The next step is to look for an escape; one partner begins a flirtation with someone else in the hope of gaining more attention.

Some people are incapable of falling in love with one person; they fall in love with two at the same time. They thus feel free; they can escape from one to the other, and never undertake the full responsibilities of love. Both means neither.

There are other people who invent a romantic, ideal, or unattainable love; they can thus luxuriate in their feelings without the necessity of approaching a partner in reality. A high ideal of love can also be used to exclude all possibilities, because no one will be found who can live up to it.

Many men, and especially many women, through mistakes in their development, have trained themselves to dislike and reject their sexual role. They have hindered their natural functions and are physically not capable, without treatment, of accomplishing a successful marriage. This is what I have called the masculine protest, and it is very much provoked by the overvaluation of men in our present culture.

If children are left in doubt of their sexual role, they are very apt to feel insecure. So long as the masculine role is taken to be the dominant role, it is natural that they should feel, whether they are boys or girls, that the masculine role is enviable. They will doubt their own ability to fulfill this role, will overstress the importance of being manly, and will try to avoid being put to the test.

This dissatisfaction with the sexual role is very frequent in our culture. We can suspect it in all cases of frigidity in women and psychic impotence in men. In these cases there is a resistance to love and marriage and a resistance in the right place. It is impossible to avoid these failures unless we truly have the feeling that men and women are equal. So long as one half of the human race has reason to be dissatisfied with the position accorded to it, we shall have a very great obstacle to the success of marriage. The remedy here is training for equality; and we should never permit children to remain ambiguous about their own future role.

I believe that the intimate devotion of love and marriage is best secured if there have not been sexual relations before the marriage. I have found that secretly most men do not really like it if their sweetheart is able to give herself before marriage. Sometimes they regard it as a sign of easy virtue and are shocked by it. Moreover, in this state of our culture, if there are intimate relations before marriage the burden is heavier for the girl.

It is also a great mistake if a marriage is contracted out of fear and not out of courage. We can understand that courage is one side of co-operation and if men and women choose their partners out of fear it is a sign that they do not wish for a real co-operation. This also holds good when they choose partners who are drunkards or very far below them in social status or in education. They are afraid of love and marriage and wish to establish a situation in which their partner will look up to them.

Friendship and Occupation

One of the ways in which social interest can be trained is through friendship. We learn in friendship to look with the eyes of another person, to listen with his ears, and to feel with his heart. If a child is frustrated, if he is always watched and guarded, if he grows up isolated, without comrades and friends, he does not develop this ability to identify himself with another person. He always thinks himself the most important being in the world and is always anxious to secure his own welfare. Training in friendship is a preparation for marriage. Games might be useful if they were regarded as a training in co-operation; but in children's games we find too often competition and the desire to excel. It is very useful to establish situations in which two children work together, study together, and learn together. I believe that we should not undervalue dancing. Dancing is a type of activity in which two people have to accomplish a common task, and I think it is good for children to be trained in dancing. I do not exactly mean the dancing we have today, where we have more of a show than of a common task. If, however, we had simple and easy dances for children, it would be a great help for their development.

Another problem that also helps to show us the preparation for marriage is the problem of occupation. Today the solution of this problem is put before the solution of love and marriage. One partner, or both, must be occupied so that they can earn their living and support a family, and we can understand that the right preparation for marriage includes also the right preparation for work.

COURTSHIP AND SEXUAL ATTRACTION[21]

We can always find the degree of courage and the degree of capacity to co-operate in the approach to the other sex. Every individual has his characteristic approach, his characteristic gait and temperament in wooing; and this is always congruous with his style of life. In this amative temperament we can see whether he says "Yes" to the future of mankind, is confident and co-operative, or whether he is interested only in his own person, suffers from stage fright, and tortures himself with the questions, "What sort of a show am I making?" "What do they think of me?" A man may be slow and cautious in wooing, or rash and precipitate; in any case, his amative temperament fits in with his goal and his style of life, and is only one expression of it. We cannot judge a man's fitness for marriage entirely by his courtship, for there he has a direct goal before him, and in other ways he may be indecisive. Nevertheless, we can gather from it sure indications of his personality.

In our own cultural conditions (and only in these conditions) it is generally expected that the man should be the first to express attraction, that the man should make the first approach. So long as this cultural demand exists, therefore, it is necessary to train boys in the masculine attitude—to take the initiative, not to hesitate or look for an escape. They can be trained, however, only if they feel themselves to be a part of the whole social life and accept its advantages and disadvantages as their own. Of course, girls and women are also engaged in wooing, they also take the initiative; but in our prevailing cultural conditions, they feel obliged to be more reserved, and their wooing is expressed in their whole gait and person, in the way they dress, the way they look, speak, and listen. A man's approach, therefore, may be called simpler and shallower, a woman's deeper and more complicated.

The sexual attraction toward the other partner is necessary, but it should always be molded along the line of a desire for

[21] Reprinted from A1931b, pp. 278–80.

human welfare. If the partners are really interested in each other, there will never be the difficulty of sexual attraction coming to an end. This stop implies always a lack of interest; it tells us that the individual no longer feels equal, friendly, and co-operative toward his partner, no longer wishes to enrich the life of his partner.

People may think, sometimes, that the interest continues but the attraction has ceased. This is never true. Sometimes the mouth lies or the head does not understand; but the functions of the body always speak the truth. If the functions are deficient, it follows that there is no true agreement between these two people. They have lost interest in each other. One of them, at least, no longer wishes to solve the task of love and marriage but is looking for an evasion and escape.

In one other way the sex drive in human beings is different from that among other beings. It is continuous. This is another way in which the welfare and continuance of humanity is guaranteed; it is a way by which humanity can increase, become numerous, and secure its welfare and survival by the greatness of its numbers. In other creatures life has taken other means to ensure this survival: In many, for example, we find that the females produce a very great number of eggs that never come to maturity. Many of them get lost or destroyed, but the great number insures that some of them always survive.

With human beings also, one method of surviving is to have children. We shall find, therefore, that in this problem of love and marriage, those people who are most spontaneously interested in the welfare of humanity are the most likely to have children, and those who are not interested, consciously or unconsciously, in their fellow beings, refuse the burden of procreation. If they are always demanding and expecting, never giving, they do not like children. They are interested in only their own persons, and they regard children as bothers, troubles, nuisances, things that will prevent them from keeping their interest in themselves. We can say, therefore, that for a full solution of the problem of love and marriage a decision to have children is necessary. A good marriage is the best means we know for bringing up the future generation of humanity, and marriage should always have this in view.

THE CASE FOR MONOGAMY[22]

The solution of the problem of love and marriage in our practical and social life is monogamy. Anyone who starts the relation that demands such an intimate devotion, such an interest in another person, cannot shake the fundamental basis of this relation, and search for an escape.

Task Orientation

We know that there is the possibility that there will be a break in the relation. Unfortunately, we cannot always avoid it. But it is easiest to avoid if we regard marriage and love as a social task that confronts us, a task that we are expected to solve. We shall then try every means to solve the problem. Breaks generally happen because the partners are not collecting all their powers. They are not creating the marriage; they are only waiting to receive something. If they face the problem in this way, of course they will fail before it. It is a mistake to regard love and marriage as if they were a paradise; and it is a mistake, too, to regard marriage as if it were the end of a story. When two people are married, the possibilities of their relationship begin; during marriage they are faced with the real tasks of life and the real opportunity to create for the sake of society.

The other point of view of marriage as an end, as a final goal, is much too prominent in our culture. We can see it, for example, in thousands of novels, in which we are left with a man and a woman, just married and really at the beginning of their life together. Yet the situation is often treated as if marriage itself had solved everything satisfactorily, as if they were at the end of their task.

[22] Reprinted from A1931b, pp. 280–86.

Another point important to realize is that love by itself does not settle everything. There are all kinds of love, and it is better to rely upon work, interest, and co-operation to solve the problems of marriage.

There is nothing at all miraculous in this whole relationship. The attitude of every individual toward marriage is one of the expressions of his style of life: we can understand it if we understand the whole individual, not unless. It is coherent with all his efforts and aims. We shall be able to find out, therefore, why so many people are always looking for a relief or escape. I can tell exactly how many people have this attitude: all the people who remain pampered children.

This is a dangerous type in our social life—these grown-up pampered children who, as part of their style of life, fixed in the first four or five years, always have the schema of apperception: "Can I get all I want?" If they can't get everything they want, they think life is purposeless. "What is the use of living," they ask, "if I cannot have what I want?" They become pessimistic: They conceive a "death wish." They make themselves sick and neurotic, and out of their mistaken style of life construct a philosophy. They feel that their mistaken ideas are of unique and tremendous importance. They feel that it is a piece of spite on the part of the universe if they have to repress their drives and emotions. They are trained in this way.

Once they experienced a favorable time in which they obtained everything they wanted. Some of them, perhaps, still feel that if they cry long enough, if they protest enough, if they refuse co-operation, they will obtain their own desires. They do not look to the coherence of life but to their own personal interests.

The result is, they do not want to contribute, they always wish to have things easy, they want to be refused nothing; and therefore they wish to have marriage itself on trial or return, they want companionate marriages, trial marriages, easier divorces: at the very beginning of marriage they demand freedom and a right to unfaithfulness. Now, if one human being is really interested in another, he must have all the characteristics belonging to that interest; he must be true, a good friend; he must feel responsible, he must make himself faithful and trustworthy. I believe that at the least a human being who has not succeeded in accomplishing such a love life or such a marriage should understand that on this point his life has been a mistake.

It is necessary, too, to be interested in the welfare of the children; and if a marriage is based upon different outlooks from the one I have supported, there are great difficulties for the bringing up of children. If the parents quarrel and look on their marriage as a trifle, if they do not see it as if its problems could be solved and the relationship could be continued successfully, it is not a very favorable situation for helping the children to be sociable.

Inappropriate Aims and Approaches

Probably there are reasons why people should not live together; probably there are cases where it would be better that they should be apart. Who should decide the case? Are we going to put it in the hands of people who themselves are not rightly taught, who themselves do not understand that marriage is a task, who themselves are interested only in their own persons? They would look at divorce in the same way as they look at marriage: "What can be gotten out of it?" These are obviously not the people to decide.

You will see very often that people divorce and remarry again and again and always make the same mistake. Then who ought to decide? Perhaps we might imagine that if something is wrong with a marriage, a psychiatrist should decide whether or not it should be broken. There is difficulty there. I do not know whether it holds true of America, but in Europe I have found that psychiatrists for the most part think that personal welfare is the most important point. Generally, therefore, if they are consulted in such a case, they recommend a sweetheart or a lover and think that this might be the way to solve the problem. I am sure that in time they will change their minds and cease to give such advice. They can only propose such a solution if they have not been rightly trained in the whole coherence of the problem, the way it hangs together with the other tasks of our life on this earth; and it is this coherence that I have been wishing to offer for your consideration.

A similar mistake is made when people look upon marriage as a solution for a personal problem. Here again I cannot speak of America, but I know that in Europe, if a boy or girl becomes neurotic, psychiatrists often advise them to have sweethearts and to begin sex relations. They advise adults, also, in the same way. This is really making love and marriage into a mere patent medicine, and these individuals are bound to lose very greatly.

The right solution of the problem of love and marriage belongs to the highest fulfillment of the whole personality. There is no problem more closely involved with happiness and a true and useful expression in life. We cannot treat it as a trifle.

We cannot look on love and marriage as a remedy for a criminal career, for drunkenness or neurosis. A neurotic needs to have the right treatment before he is fitted for love and marriage; and if he enters them before he is capable of approaching them rightly, he is bound to run into new dangers and misfortunes. Marriage is too high an ideal, and the solution of the task demands too much of our effort and creative activity for us to load it with such additional burdens.

In other ways, also, marriage is entered into with inappropriate aims. Some people marry for the sake of economic security; they marry because they pity someone; or they marry to secure a servant. There is no place for such jokes in marriage. I have even known cases where people have married to increase their difficulties. A young man, perhaps, is in difficulties about his examinations or his future career. He feels that he may very easily fail, and if he fails he wishes to be able to excuse himself. He takes on the additional task of marriage, therefore, in order to have an alibi.

I am sure we should not try to depreciate or diminish this problem but to set it on a higher level. In all the reliefs I have heard proposed, it is always the women really who bear the disadvantage. There is no question but that men in our culture already have an easier time. This is a mistake in our common approach. It cannot be overcome by a personal revolt. Especially in marriage itself, a personal revolt would disturb the social relationship and the interest of the partner. It can only be overcome by recognizing and changing the whole attitude of our culture.

A pupil of mine, Professor Rasey of Detroit, made a study and found that 42 per cent of the girls she questioned would like to have been boys; this means that they were disappointed with their own sex.[23] Can it be easy to solve the problems of love and marriage while nearly half of mankind is disappointed and discouraged, does not agree with its position, and objects to the greater freedom of the other half? Can it be easy to solve them if women are always expecting to be slighted and believe themselves to be only sexual objects for men, or believe it is natural for men to be polygamous and unfaithful?

Conclusion

From all we have said we can draw a simple, obvious, and helpful conclusion. Human beings are neither polygamous nor monogamous. But to realize that we live on this planet, in association with human beings equal to ourselves, and di-

[23] Marie I. Rasey (1887–1957), professor of educational psychology, Wayne University, Detroit, studied with Adler in Vienna during the summers of 1928 and 1929 (Rasey, 1953, pp. 160–63). Rasey (1947) reports: "Data were secured from responses to the question: 'If you had the wishing ring and could be what you liked, would you stay what you are or would you change your sex?'" (pp. 117–18). The findings were as shown in the following table. Note the girls' decreasing dissatisfaction with their sex, over the years.

	1924 N=6,000		June 1939 N=2,000		Nov. 1939 N=2,000	
	boys	girls	boys	girls	boys	girls
Stay what I am	100%	62%	99%	72%	95%	75%
Would change sex	0%	38%	1%	28%	5%	25%

vided into two sexes, and that we must solve the three problems of life that our circumstances set us in a sufficient way, will help us to see that the fullest and highest development of the individual in love and marriage can best be secured by monogamy.

Letter to a Daughter on Her Marriage

[A letter by Adler congratulating his eldest daughter, Valentine, and her husband on the occasion of their wedding may serve practically as a summary of this section. The letter is taken from the Adler biography by Phyllis Bottome (1957, p. 111). It epitomizes in the first part in a touchingly warm, personal way Adler's recommendations for a successful marriage. The second part shows equal parental concern in dealing with some very practical matters, but was not considered relevant here.]

Dear Vali and Dear Georgey:

I send you my fondest greetings and take you in my arms and congratulate you with all my heart! My thoughts are always with you.

Do not forget that married life is a task at which both of you must work, with joy.

Remember that the monogamous form of life means the finest flower of sex culture.

I ask you to fill yourselves with the brave resolve to think more about each other than about yourself, and always try to live in such a way that you make the other's life easier and more beautiful.

Don't allow either of you to become subordinate to the other. No one can stand this attitude. Don't allow anyone else to gain influence over the shaping of your marriage relation. Only make friends with people who have a sincere affection for you both. . . .

Many kisses and greetings,
Papa

ESSAY: MASCULINE PROTEST *VS.* LIBIDO

A presentation of Adler's theories of sexuality must come to grips with those of Freud, in opposition to which Adler developed them. The controversy centered around Adler's concept of "masculine protest," which represents the core difference between Freud's and Adler's psychologies altogether. It is the subject matter of the selections of Chapter 2, which were written between 1910 and 1912. The controversy found its forum until February 1911 in the weekly meetings of the Vienna Psychoanalytic Society.

One way of formulating this core difference is to say that Freud's was a physicalistic drive psychology founded on the concept of "libido," whereas Adler's was a humanistic value psychology. For Freud, sex was the most important drive, whereas for Adler it was only one important drive among others, all drives being subordinated to man's evaluation and utilization of them for his purposes.

Adler saw man's dominant purpose or goal as the attempt to overcome inferiorities and difficulties, to be strong and powerful, and to be successful according to the individual's own unique definition of what represents success. At first this presented itself to Adler, as he saw it in his patients, as "wanting to be like a man," not a woman, to be "masculine," not "feminine." For this overriding desire Adler coined the term "masculine protest."

Both parts of this term require further explanation. "To protest" as used here is synonymous not only with "to object," as the term is usually used, but also with "to assert." And "masculine" has little to do with the physiological sex characteristics of the male. Rather it refers to the preferred status of the male over the female in the general culture, and how the individual reacts to this. The culture has created entire syndromes of positive and negative traits for "masculine" and "feminine," respectively, and these have become particularly significant to the neurotic.

In a paper entitled "On the Masculine Attitude in Female Neurotics," Adler (1911c) stated in the opening paragraph: "I regard as the main motive force (*Motor*) in neurotic disease—the masculine protest against feminine or apparently feminine stirrings and sensations" (p. 74). Beginning with the second reprinting of this paper in 1924, Adler preceded this by the previously not translated paragraph on the inferiority-superiority dynamics.

"No person can simply tolerate the feeling of a real or apparent inferiority. Wherever we observe inferiority feelings we also find feelings of protest and vice versa. The *will* itself, insofar as it precedes actions . . . always moves in the direction from 'below' to 'above,' which of course at times becomes apparent only through a consideration of the context (*Zusammenhangsbetrachtung*)" (p. 74).

The following passages from Kant, which were introduced in the 1924 edition as preambles, were also not previously translated.

> The craving to dominate (*Herrschsucht*) originates in the fear of being dominated by others and aims at gaining in good time the advantage of power over them.
>
> When refined luxury has reached a certain level, a woman will turn out to be modest only by mistake and will not conceal wishing that she would rather be a man: Then she could give greater and more refined scope to her inclinations. But no man would want to be a woman.
>
> —Kant, *Anthropologie*

Importance and Transitoriness of the Term

Importance. When Adler coined the term "masculine protest" it was rather well suited to focus on the main difference between himself and Freud. With Freud sex was the all-important biological phenomenon, represented by libido and its repression. With Adler sex appeared to be such an important factor in neurotics because of the culturally determined status difference between the sexes, with the resulting fear that one may not live up to one's sexual or gender role in the case of a man, and dissatisfaction with one's assigned sexual role in the case of a woman. "Behind what one sees as sexual, there are concealed far more important relationships that merely take on the guise of sexuality—that is, the masculine protest" (A1911i, p. 149).

Adler (A1910n) introduced the term before the Vienna Psychoanalytic Society with the words: "It is a question of what the neurotic understands by 'masculine' and 'feminine.' It turns out that by 'feminine' he understands almost anything that is bad, certainly anything inferior. . . . Everything that is active is regarded as being masculine, everything passive as feminine" (p. 425). "The effort to get rid of these 'feminine' traits is experienced as 'masculine.' . . . In neurotics, the *masculine protest*, this protest of masculinity, can always be shown to be present" (p. 426).

The term is then a metaphor for human value striving in neurosis. Adler (A1911h) designated it as "the *primum movens*" (p. 111) of what he had a few years earlier described as the "aggression drive" (A1908b), by which he had meant not only hostility, but also an inertia-initiative continuum, as aggression was later understood by George Kelly (1955, pp. 508–10; 1963, p. 143), although Adler did not explicitly make this point.

When Adler introduced the masculine protest he thereby replaced the aggression drive, giving, as we read in Chapter 2, the following important explanation: "The conception of the aggression drive . . . suffered from the defect of being a biological one and not suitable to a complete understanding of neurotic phenomena. To this end, one must consider a conception of the neurotic . . . that does not admit of definition in biological terms, but only in psychological terms, or in terms of cultural psychology" (p. 37).

Transitoriness. At first Adler likened "masculine protest" to Nietzsche's "will to power," considering his own concept actually more inclusive. But the term is not really suited to such a broad meaning. The phenomenon is possible only in a social order of male dominance. As Valentine Adler (1925), Adler's daughter, pointed out: "With the destruction of male dominance, the male-female power problem disappears and with it its dialectical transformation, the 'masculine protest'" (p. 307). Thus over the years Adler (A1928k) limited masculine protest to "a frequent special case" of the general "upward striving, the will to power . . . a form of the striving for superiority" (p. 28). About this striving Adler (A1956b) then wrote: "All our functions follow its direction. They strive for conquest, security, increase, either in the right or in the wrong direction. The impetus from minus to plus never ends. The urge from below to above never ceases. Whatever premises all our philosophers and psychologists dream of—self-preservation, pleasure principle, equalization —all these are but vague representations, attempts to express the great upward drive" (p. 103).

The "frequent special case" to which Adler (A1933b) limited masculine protest was the "attitude on the part of woman, of protest against her sexual role, . . . a superiority complex based on the inferiority complex—only a girl" (p. 64). Yet the term remains strongly connected with Adler's intellectual development and some of his most important conceptions.

Adler generally did not announce changes in theory and terminology. Sometimes he even expressed himself as if his earlier views had never existed. In a passage from the complete edition of this book (p. 238), he accuses his critics of quite misunderstanding him. He states: "There are still some writers who, in order to quickly dispose of Individual Psychology, see in the 'masculine protest' the beginning and end of our views. They do not understand that the 'masculine protest' represents only one, although an important, concretization of the formal striving for superiority." In all fairness, Adler could have faulted his critics only for not having kept up with his development since 1911 which included his quiet limitation of the meaning and usage of the term masculine protest, and introduction of additional terms.

"Will to Power" and Its Misunderstandings

The introduction of Nietzsche's "will to power" by Adler in connection with masculine protest immediately led to the misunderstanding–which still exists–that Adler believed that a striving for power over others was the general human dynamic and that he actually advocated such striving. Yet Adler saw such striving for power only in the neurotic and strongly opposed it in favor of co-operation. [Incidentally, according to Walter Kaufmann (1974), for Nietzsche also the will to power "is essentially a striving to transcend and perfect oneself" (p. 248), rather than to dominate over others.]

Adler deplored (A1928m) that "today we have constructed our guiding ideal still too little in accordance with social interest and too much in accordance with personal power. . . . The striving for personal power is a disastrous delusion and poisons man's living together. Whoever desires the human community must renounce the striving for power over others" (pp. 168–69).

Adler made repeated efforts to correct the misunderstanding about his use of "will to power." In the Introduction to the second edition of *The Neurotic Constitution,* seven years after the first, he saw the necessity to counteract "meaningless talk": "The serious reader will, I hope . . . with me . . . regard each human psyche in a self-consistent progression toward a goal of perfection, so that movements, character traits, and symptoms point invariably beyond themselves. These insights will burden him with a life task: to show the way in the reduction of the striving for personal power and in the education toward the community" (A1928k, p. iv).

Three years later, in the Introduction to the third edition, Adler once more asserted: "The views of Individual Psychology demand the unconditional reduction of the striving for power and the development of social interest. The watchword of Individual Psychology is the fellow man and the fellow-man attitude toward the immanent demands of human society" (A1928k, p. vi).

Ten years later we read: "Regarding the striving for power, we find the misunderstanding that Individual Psychology not only regards psychological life as the striving for power, but propagates this idea. This striving for power is not our madness, it is what we find in others" (A1956b, p. 113). "The striving of each actively moving individual is toward overcoming, not toward power. . . . Striving for power—better, for personal power—represents only one of a thousand types, all of which seek perfection, a security-giving plus situation" (A1956b, p. 114).

The development of the concept of power in Adlerian theory has been traced by Kurt Adler (1972).

Psychological Hermaphroditism

Adler (A1910c) introduced the term "masculine protest" in a paper on "psychological hermaphroditism" (see Chapter 2), which thereupon became his most important paper.

Hermaphroditism meant the presence in each individual of biological components of the other sex, in various proportions, and was equated with bisexuality. Psychological hermaphroditism meant a corresponding presence in an individual of character traits of the other sex, depending on his sexual constitution.

Parenthetically, we should like to point out that both "hermaphroditism" and "bisexuality" have today acquired different meanings. Hermaphroditism means "a congenital condition of ambiguity of the reproductive structures so that the sex of the individual is not clearly defined as exclusively male or exclusively female" (Money and Ehrhardt, 1965, p. 285), while bisexuality means to engage in homosexual as well as heterosexual relationships.

Adler removed psychological hermaphroditism from any

direct dependence on biological factors. In contrast to Freud (1905), he held that such factors are at best only indirectly connected, and that individuals of either sex have the capacity to be more "masculine" or more "feminine" depending on which they prefer and best serves their purposes. In this view it becomes important that we live in a male-dominated culture that has created more favorable conditions and stereotypes for the male than for the female. Thus members of either sex may prefer to be "like a man" rather than "like a woman." This is the masculine protest, which in a mild form is quite widespread, while in the extreme is neurotic.

When Adler (A1910n) introduced these thoughts before the Vienna Psychoanalytic Society he believed that he was "touching upon the most delicate point in the area of psychoanalytic investigation" (p. 428), and he was right. They were exactly what led to the break with Freud, and the paper by Adler (A1910c) on this topic became the one most often referred to by Freud in his controversy with Adler.

Social Origin of the Term "Masculine Protest"

Adler considered his Individual Psychology in a sense a social psychology (A1956b, p. 157). This relationship is actually so close that he adopted the term "masculine protest" to the dynamics of the individual directly from the social scene and the woman's movement.

Adler (A1911h) explicitly stated: "The valuation of masculine and feminine in neurosis is only a crystallization of the valuation that has also existed all along in our culture and that began at the start of civilization" (p. 109). In a female patient, "*The entire armory of woman's social battle for emancipation will be found again, only distorted, altered into something senseless—that is, childish and worthless.* It is an individual battle, so to speak, a private enterprise against male prerogatives. But as an analogy, as precursor, often also as companion of the great surging social battle for equal rights for women, it shows that it originates on the way from inferiority to compensation, from the tendency to be *like a man*" (A1911c, pp. 86–87, author's italics).

Adler (A1911i) also established a connection between masculine protest and ideas of evolution (struggle for existence). In his paper before the Vienna Psychoanalytic Society at its historic meeting of February 1, 1911, he said in the Introduction (included only in the *Minutes* and not in the published full account): "The problem of the origins of protest tendencies in man and woman, and whether they exist, can be answered by referring to the development of human culture and society. It shows that these driving forces have in fact always been alive and active. The fact, among other things, that all of us have become familiar with, the idea of the struggle for existence, is evidence of this. In a similar manner, another point—that woman is devalued by man—is clearly expressed in our culture; indeed, it can even be regarded as being a driving force in our civilization. All that is needed here is to refer to the literary endeavors of the so-called antifeminists" (p. 141).

Two years before he had coined the term "masculine protest," Adler already observed: "Women are only just beginning to lead their own independent lives, apart from their family, and to develop their characters; these tendencies may constitute a certain barrier to complete merging in intercourse. This circumstance may be the reason for the particularly high incidence of [sexual] anesthesia [frigidity], in our time" (Nunberg and Federn, 1962, p. 307). Adler gave an estimate of 70 per cent of women being frigid.

Above we find: "The urge to change [woman's present condition] brings about all ideals of . . . emancipation, and degenerates in personal life into a hundred forms of the 'masculine protest' " (p. 88). But, Adler warns, the social struggle for woman's equality must not enter her personal relations. Woman's disadvantaged position is a cultural mistake. "It cannot be overcome by a personal revolt. Especially in marriage itself, a personal revolt would disturb the social relationship and the interest of the partner. The mistake can only be overcome by recognizing and changing the whole attitude of our culture" (p. 141).

In the light of all this, the question whether the woman's movement is to be understood as an extension of the masculine protest is to be answered with a definite "No." Rather the masculine protest is a miscarriage from the woman's movement into an individual woman's private life—on the generally useless side of life.

Two Examples of Masculine Protest

In this connection Adler (A1911c, p. 87) refers to Helena Racowitza (1845–1911), whose memoirs had recently been published. Her name was probably meaningful enough for Adler's readers then. But today we are perhaps justified to present her case briefly.

Helena Racowitza was the daughter of a Prussian nobleman, von Dönniges, professor of political science in Berlin, later a diplomat in the service of the King of Bavaria. As a rebellious young girl Helena succeeded through considerable perseverance in having an affair with the brilliant socialist leader Ferdinand Lassalle, twenty years her elder. This led to a duel in which Lassalle died at the hand of a second suitor, the wealthy Romanian nobleman Yanko Racowitza. Helena married the victor "for reasons she could certainly never explain to her friends. . . . She was touched, she said, by his tender devotion, his loyalty and chivalry, in refusing to accept the world's view of her relations with Lassalle" (Bonsal, 1911). A few months later, Yanko died of consumption. Helena then went on the stage, wrote several novels, married twice more, and lived altogether an adventurous life, which she ended by suicide. The affair with Lassalle was so sensational that "about one hundred volumes, including two by the heroine" (Bonsal, 1911) were written on the subject.

In her memoirs, Racowitza (1910) writes of "equality of the sexes" (p. 29) and may give the impression of standing for the emancipation of women. But soon a wanting to be "like a man" becomes apparent. As a twelve-year-old she suggested to a newlywed friend who complained about the sexual escapades of her husband, "Why don't you do the same?" (p. 29), and she remembered distinctly that on this day "the foundation was laid to all my future life" (p. 28). The following passage shows that she was indeed fighting an "individual battle" for personal triumphs and humiliation of the opponent. "I always demanded and obtained from my admirers unequivocal recognition of the superior qualities of their favored rivals. In Yanko's case, when he at first refused to study Lassalle's works with me, I said, 'You must. You owe it to yourself. You ought to know how great is the intellect of the man I prefer to you, for when you recognize the superiority of his mind your pride will no longer suffer'" (p. 79). One sees her lack of compassion, her desire for "childish and worthless" triumphs, her lust to dominate and humiliate.

Adler (A1912a, p. 176) mentioned these memoirs once more, this time together with those of Marie Bashkirtseva (1889), as "mostly refined descriptions of all these attempts of masculine protest" (p. 176). By birth a Russian noblewoman, Bashkirtseva (1860–84) was a brilliant girl with many-sided gifts who by the age of twenty had become a naturalistic painter of some renown in Paris. She died of tuberculosis at the age of twenty-four. Her memoirs show her original great ambition to make something of her talents, and become very moving reading as she faces death. But her case does not seem quite so striking.

Social-Psychological and Philosophical Origins of Other Concepts

The derivation of "masculine protest" from the social scene was only one aspect of Adler's general position of regarding psychology as a social and cultural science–not primarily a biological science in the mechanistic sense–regardless of his *Study of Organ Inferiority and Its Psychical Compensation* (A1907a). Ironically, Freud held against him exactly: "Instead of psychology, Adler's doctrine presents, in large part, biology" (A1911i, p. 147). Or, earlier, "Adler subjects the psychological material too soon to biological points of view" (Nunberg and Federn, 1967, p. 432).

Adler (A1956b, p. 92) objected to Freud's use of metaphors from physics and mechanics. Since man is not a machine, such metaphors cannot do justice to the subject matter. Instead, Adler borrowed his terms and metaphors from social life and the social sciences. The group is composed of individuals; therefore, what becomes apparent there should also be valid for the individual. The following are some of Adler's concepts that can be traced to social scientists.

Subjective evaluation of objective facts. When Adler (A1920a) stated, "More important than disposition, objective experience, and environment is the subjective evaluation of these. Furthermore, this evaluation stands in a certain, often strange, relation to reality" (p. 4); he compared this to the concept of the "ideological superstructure over the economic foundation" of Marx and Engels. However, in mass psychology the facts created by the ideological superstructure "enforce a leveling of the individual differences" (p. 4). These passages referring to Marx and Engels are, incidentally, not included in the English edition of *Practice and Theory of Individual Psychology.*

Creative power of the individual. The subjective evaluation that is to a considerable extent free from the objective reality is attributed by Adler to the "creative power" (*schöpferische Kraft*) of the individual. This was Adler's answer to any absolute determinism. He credited Heymann Steinthal (1823–99), an early social psychologist, for having "presented the psyche as organic creative power" (A1920a, p. 85), only that Steinthal used *Gestaltungskraft,* a synonym for *schöpferische Kraft.*

Oversensitivity. Oversensitivity (*Ueberempfindlichkeit*) is important in Adler's description of the neurotic disposition. The patient with increased inferiority feelings easily "considers himself neglected, hurt, small, or besmudged" (A1956b, p. 290). Adler credits Karl Lamprecht (1856–1915), cultural historian, for having observed such sensitivity (*Reizsamkeit*) in the psychology of nations (*Völkerpsychologie*).

Life style. This term, which became so prominent in

Adler's later writings–that is, after 1926–was most likely indirectly suggested to him by Max Weber (1864–1920), German sociologist and politician. Weber meant by this term the life style of a group or subculture. Thus when Adler introduced the term, he specified it at first as "individual life style" (see Ansbacher, 1967). Continuing the parallel between culture and individual, Powers (1973) has shown that as myths provide a key to the understanding of a culture or group life style, so an individual's early recollections provide a key to the understanding of his individual life style.

Symptoms as safeguards of self-esteem. With regard to his insight that laziness, for example, and really all inhibiting neurotic symptoms can be understood as devices by the patient to safeguard his self-esteem, Adler (A1920a) refers to German historian Barthold G. Niebuhr (1776–1831). He quotes from Niebuhr's *Roman History,* Vol. 3: "National vanity, like the personal variety, is more ashamed of failure that betrays limitation of power, than of the greatest disgrace that follows from lazy and cowardly omission of any effort. By the former arrogant claims are destroyed, in case of the latter they continue" (p. 71). In Adler's (A1956b) own terms this becomes: "Lazy children are like tight-rope walkers with a net underneath the rope; when they fall, they fall softly. It is less painful to be told that one is lazy than that one is incapable. . . . Laziness serves as a screen to hide the child's lack of faith in himself, prohibiting him from making attempts to cope with the problems confronting him" (p. 391).

Various concepts. As a social psychologist, Adler was also a philosophical psychologist, philosophy being a part of the humanities in contrast to the natural sciences, and he gladly acknowledged his debt to philosophers. (This again is in contrast to Freud who, for example, denied any knowledge of Nietzsche when certain similarities in thinking were pointed out to him [Nunberg and Federn, 1962, pp. 359–60].) Adler took *"Everything depends on one's opinion . . ."*–the motto for his first major book (A1912a)–from the leading Stoic philosopher Seneca. "Will to power" was, of course, borrowed from Nietzsche. The concept of *purposive adaptation* was strengthened in Adler, and the value of *fictions* in this process was suggested to him by the work of German pragmatist philosopher Vaihinger (1911b), who became particularly significant for Adler. *Early recollections* as a diagnostic tool was clarified for Adler by French pragmatist Bergson (Ansbacher, 1973). For the concept of a unified *life plan,* which for many years preceded the concept of life style, Adler acknowledged partial accord with the important teachings of Steinthal, Vaihinger, and Bergson (A1913h; in the later printings Steinthal is omitted). *Common sense* vs. *private intelligence* as descriptive of mental health vs. mental disorder was most likely accepted by Adler from Kant (Ansbacher, 1965). Adler's understanding of the three main conditions of our lives (on this earth, in social interaction, and in sexual dimorphism) as *life tasks* (*Aufgaben*) is in accord with the neo-Kantian Hermann Cohen, who considered that in man everything that is *gegeben* ("given") is really *aufgegeben* ("propounded") like a riddle or a task (Vleeschauwer, 1974). Finally, Adler's concept of *social interest* or social feeling (*Gemeinschaftsgefühl*) had its forerunner in John Stuart Mill's "fellow feeling" and "social feelings of mankind, the desire to be in unity with our fellow creatures" (Ansbacher, 1968, p. 140).

Beyond belonging to the social sciences, Adler's sources share a common ground from which Ellenberger (1970) concluded quite correctly: "Adler definitely belongs to the philosophy of the Enlightenment, with his emphasis that man is a rational and a social being, endowed with free will and the ability to make conscious decisions" (p. 629).

Dialectical Dynamics

As stated above, Adler replaced the concept of "aggression drive" with that of "masculine protest," because he wanted a conception that would not be expressed in biological terms "but only in psychological terms, or in terms of cultural psychology" (pp. 37, 145). He wanted to express himself not in terms of a mechanistic natural science, but in social science terms. Drive is a mechanistic concept; machines neither protest nor strive.

Bipolar conception. Typical for a mechanistic concept, a "drive" is *unipolar*—that is, it is simply a force that is applied, and nothing else. It is a *demonstrative,* positivistic conception. On the other hand, a "protest" is a solemn declaration of opinion, usually of dissent or objection, although it may also be an assertion. "Opinion" implies that different views regarding the same subject matter are possible about which one may dispute. Thus "protest" is a *dialectical* conception and is also *bipolar,* as we shall see. Rychlak (1968) has shown in detail that these two conceptions represent two philosophies of science and that "Dialectical terminology presents us with the *most accurate* picture of the fundamental human condition" (p. 255).

A dialectical conception is bipolar in that it includes a thesis and an antithesis. But it includes also a third, uniting factor, namely the common point of reference of the first two, or how their antagonism may be resolved, the synthesis. When Adler (A1910c) introduced the concept of "masculine protest," he specified these three factors as follows: "(A) Traits evaluated as feminine. (B) Hypertrophied masculine protest. (C) Compromise formation between A and B." While Adler soon gave up the terms "feminine," "masculine," and "masculine protest" for his dialectical dynamic conception, he retained its structure and meaning.

Point A was in turn designated as inferiority feelings, normal or intensified; feelings of insecurity, weakness, or being "below"; or a felt "minus position."

Point B received the largest number of successive names: wanting to be a real man, wanting power, or wanting to attain a goal of power, superiority, success, perfection, completion, a "plus situation."

Point C became the movement, the striving toward these goals, a continuous overcoming of difficulties, compensation, or, in mental disorder, a construction of additional difficulties (the symptoms) as excuses for not reaching one's goals out of fear of failure, while still saving a vestige of one's self-esteem.

In the same year, although not so precisely, Adler (A1910f) expressed the dialectical structure in terms of (a) inferiority feelings, (b) psychological compensation tendencies, and (c) corresponding behavior and attitudes. The passage in question reads: "A basic psychological law is the dialectical reversal of organ inferiority via a subjective inferiority feeling into psychological tendencies of compensation and overcompensation. However, this is not a natural law, but a general, plausible seduction of the human mind. The behavior and attitudes of the child who is thus neurotically disposed show clearly the traces of this dialectical reversal, very early in childhood" (p. 54).

The dialectical dynamic is described by Adler (A1929d) particularly well in the following, where it is also tied in with the concepts of the past and the future. "The future is tied up with our striving and with our goal, while the past represents the state of inferiority or inadequacy that we are trying to overcome. This is why . . . we should not be astonished if in the cases where we see an inferiority complex we find a superiority complex more or less hidden. On the other hand, if we inquire into a superiority complex . . . we can always find a more or less hidden inferiority complex. . . . If we look at things this way, it takes away the apparent paradox of two contradictory tendencies . . . existing in the same individual. For it is obvious that as normal sentiments the striving for superiority and the feeling of inferiority are naturally complementary. We should not strive to be superior and to succeed if we did not feel a certain lack in our present condition. . . . The striving for superiority never ceases. It constitutes in fact the mind, the psyche of the individual" (pp. 27–28).

Acknowledgment of Hegel and Nietzsche. As Adler formed dialectical, bipolar conceptions, he also acknowledged Hegel (1770–1831), dialectician and teacher of Marx. When in 1907 he addressed the Philosophical Society at the University of Vienna on organ inferiority and compensation, and explained Freud's concept of repression as a restraint on "unsuitable or immature methods of overcompensation," Adler (A1908e) pointed out: "The fact that in this process [of overcompensation] a character trait, drive, wish, or concept may fall into its opposite—that is, may express itself by its antithesis—is a special case reminding one to some extent of Hegelian dialectics" (p. 31). In 1909 Adler credited Hegel with having "enabled the idea of evolution to make a breakthrough in philosophy" by placing "in the foreground of his philosophy his conception of dialectics—that is, the transformation of one thing into its opposite, of the thesis into the antithesis—matters that occupy us continuously" (Nunberg and Federn, 1967, pp. 333–34). The following year, 1910, Adler introduced his concept of masculine protest—a dialectical construction, as we have seen.

As to "the idea of evolution," Hegel had asserted that "it is possible for something to both be and not be when it is in the process of 'becoming'" (Rychlak, 1968, pp. 286–87). The "becoming" was one of the great concerns of Adler, from the beginning and throughout his life. Thus he quoted on the final page of *The Neurotic Constitution* from the minor German philosopher Rudolph Hildebrand (1824–94): "Through the great *being* that surrounds and deeply penetrates us, there extends a great *becoming* that strives toward the perfect *being*" (A1917, p. 445; see also Ansbacher, 1962).

At the time of his first acknowledgment of Hegel—that is, in 1908—Adler expressed also great admiration for Nietzsche (1844–1900). "Among all great philosophers . . . Nietzsche is closest to our way of thinking. . . . In Nietzsche's work, one finds almost on every page observations reminiscent of those we make in therapy" (Nunberg and Federn, 1962, p. 358). This affinity also rested largely on dialectics. According to Walter Kaufmann (1974, p. 84), Nietzsche was more consistently dialectical even than Hegel. Thus Adler could easily make the transition from the masculine protest to Nietzsche's "will to power." "'I want to be a real man' is the guiding fiction in every neurosis, for which it claims greater reality value than the normal psyche. . . . Nietzsche's 'will to power' . . . includes much of our conception." That "will to power" did not mean essentially power over others but wanting to be strong, able to overcome obstacles, including one's own weaknesses, was discussed earlier.

Teleological principle. Important for both Nietzsche and Adler is the teleological principle—that is, not to look for causes of behavior in the past but for goals in the future. Nietzsche (1884) phrased this principle as "Not whence you come shall henceforth constitute your honor, but whither you are going! . . . Your nobility should not look backward but ahead!" (pp. 315–16). Nietzsche's influence may be seen in Adler's (A1956b) parallel phrase: "The most important question of the healthy and the diseased mental life is not Whence? but Whither? . . . In this whither? the cause is contained" (p. 91).

Questioning attitude. Kaufmann (1974) judged Nietzsche to be "more consistently 'dialectical'" than Hegel, because Nietzsche "was . . . a far more rigorous questioner. . . . All assumptions had to be questioned" (p. 84). This is illustrated by the quotation from Nietzsche, "I am not bigoted enough for a system—and not even for my system" (p. 80). The same questioning attitude is reflected in Adler's (A1956b) statements: "We regard man as if nothing in his life were causally determined and as if every phenomenon could have been different" (p. 91), and "General rules—even those laid down by Individual Psychology, of my own creation—should be regarded as nothing more than an aid to a preliminary illumination of the field of view in which the single individual can be found—or missed" (p. 194). And finally, "Don't blindly believe any 'authority'—not even me!" (A1930e, p. 172).

With all these methodological similarities it is important to recognize that in matters of substance Adler was essentially on the opposite pole from Nietzsche. This is best reflected in their respective model of the ideal man—for Nietzsche it was an elitist "superman"; for Adler, a democratic "fellow man."

Objective reality or thought process?—Vaihinger. Regarding the dialectical method, a main issue is: Do the objective events in the physical world follow the principle of dialectics, or do only our thought processes operate in this manner?

Hegel represented the first position. As Thilly and Wood (1957) formulated it, for Hegel "the dialectical evolution of the concepts in the mind of the philosopher coincides with the objective evolution of the world; the categories of subjective thought are likewise categories of the universe; thought and being are identical" (p. 480). This of course reflects Hegel's idealism. But interestingly, especially the last phrase, "thought and being are identical," can, in reverse order, also be cited as an assertion of pure materialism.

The second alternative, that only our thought processes operate dialectically, is accepted by Nietzsche; most forcefully by Vaihinger, in whom Adler found strong support; and by Adler.

Nietzsche, according to Kaufmann (1974), did not believe "that reality is self-contradictory. Only unqualified judgments about reality involve us in superficial inconsistencies" (p. 80). Thus Nietzsche can be regarded as a "dialectical monist" (p. 235). "The metaphysics of the will to power is a dialectical monism in which the basic force is conceived as essentially creative" (p. 241).

Hans Vaihinger (1852–1933), German pragmatist, is known for his theory of fictions, his philosophy of "as if." Vaihinger's (1911b) basic assumption is that thinking is an activity for the purpose of solving problems in the real world, and that it is well suited for this purpose, while at the same time it differs from the objective processes. "The ways of thought are different from those of reality. . . . The greatest and most important human errors originate through thought processes being taken for copies of reality itself" (p. 8). Vaihinger singles out Hegel for having committed this mistake. "The Hegelian system offers historically the most glaring and typical example of this general error of philosophy: the confusion of thought processes with events, the conversion of subjective thought events into objective world-events. (That the Hegelian dialectic is, however, based on a correct insight into the nature of logical development, we shall have occasion to remark later)" (p. 8).

Vaihinger indicts Hegel for "abuse of abstractions" (p. 204), a phrase that Adler adopted. "Abstractions are a necessary aid to thought and meet a practical need, but they furnish no theoretical knowledge, twist and turn, define and differentiate them as we may. We confuse fact and fiction, means and ends, if we attempt to deduce anything from such linguistic aids" (p. 205). Vaihinger (1911a) holds that Hegel placed the contradictions that he had found in his abstractions "erroneously . . . into reality, after having made the very abstractions into realities first. It is the abuse of the abstractions that creates the disturbances through 'the most grotesque contradictions'" (p. 395).

Adler's general dialectical approach. Adler's dialectical conception extended into the various aspects of his theory and its applications, making it a remarkably integrated and self-consistent system. In the complete edition we refer to Adler's dialectics in connection with his views on human creativity and self-determination, understanding of marital conflicts, methods of problem-solving and conflict resolution, theory of neurosis, understanding of symptoms, and techniques of psychotherapy. At the same time, Adler firmly adhered to the demonstrative unity and spontaneity of the organism rejecting the assumption of objectively, firmly established categories, dichotomies, and contradictions. Thus it seems well warranted to describe Adler's approach philosophically as one of "dialectical monism," the term applied by Kaufmann (1968, p. 241) to Nietzsche.

A survey of Adler's "use of the dialectic" has been published by Robert Dolliver (1974). It is quite good, except for Dolliver's understanding of Adler's development, with which we disagree.

Joseph F. Rychlak (1968), who brought the importance of the dialectical tradition to the attention of contemporary American psychology, quotes as the hallmark of the dialectical approach the Talmudic metaphor, "Every stick has two ends" (p. 328). This metaphor is indeed appropriate for the general approach of Adler, the practitioner, and for present-day Adlerian psychologists. In fact, there is a small paper entitled "Every Stick Has Two Ends" by William Beecher (1946), a no-nonsense Adlerian and pungent writer. The paper is about a boy who after a serious illness had become increasingly dependent on his parents, so that they had actually become his slaves. Beecher reports this case as a reminder that "Too often we may grasp the wrong end of the stick. We forget that the 'weak' individual is the one who is in the stronger position. It is useless to ask him to give up such a favorable spot–as long as his 'slaves' remain willing or intimidated into his service" (p. 85).

But Rychlak (1968) apparently believes that dialectics is completely associated with dualism. He does not appreciate that one can well be a monist, in the demonstrative tradition, as far as objective reality is concerned, and at the same time a dialectician as far as the subjectivity of human psychological processes is concerned–that is, a dialectical monist. Thus Rychlak (1973) quite erroneously concludes that at heart Adler was as distrustful as Freud of dialectics, "and after he left the Freudian camp he positively opposed any oppositional type of theoretical formulation" (p. 209). Dolliver (1974) sees Adler's development the same way and even ventures the daring explanation "that Adler tried to eradicate the influence of the dialectic from his theorizing because of its association to Freud" (p. 20). Adler (1956b) did indeed continue to perfect his holistic model of human structure, removing all remnants of dualism. In fact, he declared any theory that accepts dichotomies in a positivistic sense to be unscientific (p. 229). But as far as human subjective functioning is concerned, a dialectical conception is central in Adler's theory of apperception and cognition, and in his practice of reconstructing these functions as we have attempted to show in the complete edition.

Freud's Reaction

Of the critiques brought forth and new terms introduced by Adler, Freud reacted most strongly and lastingly to "masculine protest."

At first, when Adler introduced "masculine protest" in 1910 before the Vienna Psychoanalytic Society, Freud simply rejected it with the words: "The concepts of 'masculine' and 'feminine' are of no use in psychology and we do better . . . to employ the concepts of libido and repression. Whatever is of the libido has a masculine character, and whatever is repression is of a feminine character. . . . What Adler has described is a change of nomenclature through which we lose clarity" (Nunberg and Federn, 1967, pp. 432–33).

Freud's remark is at first somewhat puzzling, yet it directly hits the crucial difference. Libido-repression refers to a presumed basic unconscious *intrapsychic* conflict expressed in highly abstract terms, while masculine-feminine refers to an *interpersonal* transactional conflict expressed more concretely. When Freud then insists that this is merely a matter of semantics, he either did not realize the full significance of his cogent formulation or tried to deny it.

Castration fear and penis envy. But Freud did not let matters rest with this simple denial. Shortly after, he adapted the masculine protest to his own system by subsuming it under the castration complex—that is, castration fear and penis envy. He succeeded with this adaptation so well that he is today often considered the originator of masculine protest. Yet the issue around the masculine protest never came to rest with Freud. For him the masculine protest became quite justly the symbolization of the controversy with Adler and continued in focus throughout his life.

Freud (1911) introduced masculine protest in his well-known paper on the Schreber case in the following: "This feminine phantasy [of Schreber's] . . . was met at once by indignant repudiation—a true 'masculine protest,' to use Adler's expression, but in a sense different from his" (p. 426). What Freud meant by this "different sense" he expressed at a meeting of the Psychoanalytic Society the same year. "In . . . neurotics who set such great store by their masculinity, . . . one can almost always succeed in tracing the neuroses to the castration complex. . . . If the castration complex is taken into consideration, it will be possible to bring a number of Adler's propositions into harmony with our views" (Nunberg and Federn, 1974, p. 275).

A few years later, Freud (1918) joined masculine protest and castration complex in his paper "The Taboo of Virginity." "Women go through an early phase in which they envy their brothers the token of maleness. . . . This 'penis envy' forms part of the castration complex. If 'masculine' is to include the connotation of 'wishing to be masculine,' the term 'masculine protest' fits this attitude; this term was coined by Alfred Adler for the purpose of proclaiming this factor as the foundation of all neurosis in general" (pp. 230–31).

The clearest statement on the matter is found in one of Freud's last papers. Freud (1937) held: "We must not be misled by the term 'masculine protest' into supposing that what the man repudiates is the *attitude* of passivity, or, as we may say, the social aspect of femininity. . . . What they reject is not passivity in general but passivity in relation to *men*. That is to say, the 'masculine protest' is in fact nothing other than fear of castration" (p. 357n).

Adler's rebuttal to this argument was from the start: "The castration fear is to be taken symbolically: The patient establishes this fear . . . to secure himself against any kind of undertaking whatsoever. . . . The castration complex . . . serves as a safety measure" (Nunberg and Federn, 1974, pp. 277–78). In other words, it becomes an obsessive idea through which the individual excuses himself from attending to socially more important matters for which he feels unprepared.

Narcissism and ego ideal. His reductionistic reinterpretation of masculine protest notwithstanding, Freud tacitly acknowledged the deeper theoretical significance of Adler's concept by introducing three years later some concepts of his own serving similar functions.

Adler's concept of masculine protest signified: (a) a present state of feminine traits, feeling inferior (thesis); (b) a goal in the future of masculine strength and superiority (antithesis); and (c) the striving and movement from (a) to (b). Whereas the end point of Freud's dynamics had been the attainment of an object to satisfy a drive, Adler's "goal" concept was an aspired future condition of the person himself, a self-ideal.

Such a concept involving a future projection of the individual was introduced by Freud (1914b) in his paper "On Narcissism." The concept was "ego ideal," which subsequently became the "super-ego." The editor of the *Standard Edition* of Freud's works, John Strachey, underlines the importance of this paper in his Introduction:

"The paper is among the most important of Freud's writings and may be regarded as one of the pivots in the evolution of his views. . . . It enters into the deeper problems of the relations between the ego and external objects, and it draws the new distinction between 'ego-libido' and 'object-libido.' Furthermore–most important of all, perhaps–it introduces the concepts of the 'ego ideal' . . . the basis of what was ultimately to be described as the 'super-ego' in *The Ego and the Id* (1923). . . . At two points . . . it trenches upon the controversies with Adler and Jung. . . . *One of Freud's motives . . . was, no doubt, to show that the concept of narcissism offers an alternative to Jung's nonsexual 'libido' and to Adler's 'masculine protest'*" (p. 70, italics added).

Summary and conclusion. Freud thought at first that Adler's "masculine protest," based on the masculine-feminine dialectics, could simply be reduced to his own main concepts at that time, "libido" and "repression." But it turned out that Freud had to develop his system further to provide an alternative for the social considerations introduced with the "masculine protest." This took over a decade, after which Freud introduced the concepts of id, ego, and super-ego, which appeared more vital than libido and repression.

We have seen, then, that Adler had a profound influence on Freud. Freud was unable "to let Adler go," as Paul Roazen (1975, p. 208) stated it. Roazen also noted that "Adler's ideas were swept up by Freud's pupils even though they may not have been aware of what they were doing" (p. 205). Adler (A1933b) had come to a very similar conclusion when he wrote: "It will appear to many as though I had unfairly anticipated the development of psychoanalysis during the past twenty-five years. I am the prisoner of psychoanalysis who does not let it go" (p. 255; new translation).

Regarding Freud's criticisms of Adler, Roazen (1975) concludes: "Contemporary analysts, if asked to defend Freud's criticism of Adler, would find themselves in an embarrassing position" (p. 204). Roazen supports this by listing concepts of Freud that have disappeared from the psychoanalytic literature and concepts of Adler that have silently been taken over.

REFERENCES

There are three lists of references: (1) to Adler, (2) by Adler to other authors, and (3) by the editors to other authors.

1. *References to Adler.* This list includes all references to Adler, made by himself or by the editors. The items are identified by "A," the year of first publication, and a letter, following the master bibliography of Adler in *Superiority and Social Interest* (A1964a, pp. 397–420). In those items from which the text includes a quotation, the original source is followed by the source from which the quotation is actually taken, where this differs. Page references in the text thus may refer to this second source.

2. *Adler's References to Other Authors.* Adler was generally very sparse with references. Most of those included in the present writings were supplied by him with his contributions to the Bethe *Handbook* (see p. 420), apparently on request from its editors. Nearly all these references were in various degrees incomplete and were completed by the present editors as far as possible. English translations are cited where such could be readily found.

3. *Editors' References to Other Authors.* We considered it helpful to keep Adler's and the editors' references to other authors distinct.

REFERENCES TO ADLER

A1905b Drei Psycho-Analysen von Zahleneinfällen und obsedierenden Zahlen (Three psychoanalyses of ideas of numbers and obsessive numbers), *Psychiatrische und neurologische Wochenschrift,* 7, 263–66.

A1907a *Studie über Minderwertigkeit von Organen* (Study of organ inferiority). Vienna: Urban & Schwarzenberg [Trans.: A1917c].

A1908b Der Aggressionstrieb im Leben und in der Neurose (The aggression drive in life and in neurosis), *Fortschritte der Medizin,* 26, 577–84; as reprinted in A1928n, pp. 33–42.

A1908e Die Theorie der Organminderwertigkeit und ihre Bedeutung für Philosophie und Psychologie (The theory of organ inferiority and its significance for philosophy and psychology), *Universität Wien, Philosophische Gesellschaft, Wissenschaftliche Beilage,* 21, 11–26; as reprinted in A1928n, pp. 24–33.

A1908f Zwei Träume einer Prostituierten (Two dreams of a prostitute), *Zeitschrift für Sexualwissenschaft,* 1, 103–6.

A1909a Über neurotische Disposition: zugleich ein Beitrag zur Ätiologie und zur Frage der Neurosenwahl (On neurotic disposition: a contribution to the etiology and problem of choice of neurosis), *Jahrbuch für Psychoanalyse und psychopathologische Forschung,* 1, 526–45; as reprinted in A1928n, pp. 59–75.

A1910c Der psychische Hermaphroditismus im Leben und in der Neurose (Psychological hermaphroditism in life and neurosis), *Fortschritte der Medizin,* 28, 486–93; as reprinted in A1928n, pp. 76–84.

A1910d Trotz und Gehorsam (Defiance and obedience), *Monatshefte für Pädagogik und Schulpolitik,* 2, 321–28; as reprinted in A1928n, pp. 84–92.

A1910f Die psychische Behandlung der Trigeminusneuralgie (The psychological treatment of trigeminus neuralgia), *Zentralblatt für Psychoanalyse,* 1, 10–20; as reprinted in A1930p, pp. 52–67.

A1910m Review of C. G. Jung, "Ueber Konflikte der kindlichen Seele" (On conflicts of the soul of the child), in *Zentralblatt für Psychoanalyse,* 1, pp. 122–23.

A1910n Psychic hermaphroditism, *Minutes of the Vienna Psychoanalytic Society;* Vol. 2, *1908–10,* ed. H. Nunberg and E. Federn (New York: International Universities Press, 1967), pp. 423–28.

A1911a Die Rolle der Sexualität in der Neurose (The role of sexuality in neurosis); in A1928n, pp. 92–100.

A1911b "Verdrängung" und "männlicher Protest": ihre Rolle und Bedeutung für die neurotische Dynamik ("Repression" and "masculine protest": their role and significance for the neurotic dynamics); in A1928n, pp. 100–9.

A1911c Über männliche Einstellung bei weiblichen Neurotikern (On masculine attitude in female neurotics), *Zentralblatt für Psychoanalyse,* 1, 174–78; as reprinted in A1930p, pp. 74–78 plus new pp. 78–97.

A1911d Beitrag zur Lehre vom Widerstand (Contribution to the theory of resistance), *Zentralblatt für Psychoanalyse,* 1, 214–19; as reprinted in A1930p, pp. 97–103.

A1911h Some problems of psychoanalysis, and discussion, *Minutes of the Vienna Psychoanalytic Society;* Vol. 3, *1910–11,* ed. H. Nunberg and E. Federn (New York: International Universities Press, 1974), pp. 102–11 (pp. 102–5, abstract of A1911a; pp. 105–11, discussion).

A1911i The masculine protest as the central problem of neurosis, and discussion, *Minutes of the Vienna Psychoanalytic Society;* Vol. 3, *1910–11,* ed. H. Nunberg and E. Federn (New York: International Universities Press, 1974), pp. 140–58, 168–77.

A1912a *Über den nervösen Charakter: Grundzüge einer vergleichenden Individual-Psychologie und Psychotherapie* (The nervous character: fundamentals of a comparative individual psychology and psychotherapy) (Wiesbaden: Bergmann), 4th ed., A1928k. [Trans. A1917a.]

A1913d Individualpsychologische Ergebnisse bezüglich Schlafstörungen (Individual-Psychological conclusions regarding sleep disturbances), *Fortschritte der Medizin,* 31, 925–33; as reprinted in A1930p, pp. 116–23.

A1913g Individualpsychologische Bemerkungen zu Alfred Bergers *Hofrat Eysenhardt* (Individual-Psychological comments on Alfred Berger's *Hofrat Eysenhardt*), *Zeitschrift für psychologische Medizin und Psychotherapie*, 5, 77–89; as reprinted in A1930p, pp. 189–99.

A1914a [Editor with Carl Furtmüller] *Heilen und Bilden: ärztlich-pädagogische Arbeiten des Vereins für Individualpsychologie* (Healing and educating: medical-educational papers of the Society for Individual Psychology) (Munich: Reinhardt); as in 3rd ed., A1928n.

A1914f Soziale Einflüsse in der Kinderstube (Social influences in the nursery), *Pädagogisches Archiv*, 56, 473–87.

A1913h Zur Rolle des Unbewussten in der Neurose (The role of the unconscious in the neurosis), *Zentralblatt für Psychoanalyse*, 3, pp. 169–74; as reprinted in A1930p, pp. 155–61.

A1917a *The neurotic constitution: outline of a comparative individualistic psychology and psychotherapy*, trans. B. Glueck and J. E. Lind, Introduction by William A. White (New York: Moffat, Yard).

A1917c *Study of organ inferiority and its psychical compensation: a contribution to clinical medicine*, trans. S. E. Jelliffe (New York: Nervous and Mental Diseases Publishing Co.).

A1920a *Praxis und Theorie der Individualpsychologie: Vorträge zur Einführung in die Psychotherapie für Ärzte, Psychologen und Lehrer* (Practice and theory of Individual Psychology: introductory lectures in psychotherapy for physicians, psychologists, and educators) (Munich: Bergmann), 4th ed., A1930p. [Trans. A1925a.]

A1925a *The practice and theory of Individual Psychology*, trans. P. Radin. (London: Routledge & Kegan Paul; reprinted, Totowa, N.J.: Littlefield, Adams, 1968).

A1925i Erörterungen zum Paragraph 144 (Discussion of paragraph 144 [making abortion illegal]), *Internationale Zeitschrift für Individualpsychologie*, 3, 338–40.

A1926a *Liebesbeziehungen und deren Störungen* (Love

relationships and their disturbances) (Vienna, Leipzig: Moritz Perles).

A1926e Psychische Einstellung der Frau zum Sexualleben (Woman's psychological attitude to sex life), *Handbuch der normalen und pathologischen Physiologie,* ed. A. Bethe et al. (Berlin: Springer), Vol. 14 (1), pp. 802–7; as reprinted in A1930d, pp. 89–97.

A1926f Psychosexuelle Haltung des Mannes (Man's psychosexual attitude), *Handbuch der normalen und pathologischen Physiologie,* ed. A. Bethe et al. (Berlin: Springer), Vol. 14 (1), pp. 808–12; as reprinted in A1930d, pp. 98–106.

A1926g Pubertätserscheinungen (Puberty phenomena), *Handbuch der normalen und pathologischen Physiologie,* ed. A. Bethe et al. (Berlin: Springer), Vol. 14 (1), pp. 842–44; as reprinted in A1930d, pp. 85–89.

A1927a *Menschenkenntnis* (Understanding human nature) (Leipzig: Hirzel) [trans. in A1927b].

A1927b *Understanding human nature,* trans. W. B. Wolfe (New York: Greenberg; reprinted, New York: Fawcett Publications, 1954).

A1928c Erotisches Training und erotischer Rückzug (Erotic training and erotic retreat), in *Verhandlungen des l. Internationalen Kongresses für Sexualforschung, Berlin, 1926,* ed. M. Marcuse (Berlin, Köln: Marcus & Webers), Vol. 3, pp. 1–7.

A1928k *Über den nervösen Charakter: Grundzüge einer vergleichenden Individual-Psychologie und Psychotherapie* (The nervous character: fundamentals of a comparative individual psychology and psychotherapy), 4th ed. (Munich: Bergmann).

A1928m Psychologie der Macht (Psychology of power), in *Gewalt und Gewaltlosigkeit: Handbuch des aktiven Pazifismus,* ed. Franz Kobler (Zurich: Rotapfel-Verlag), pp. 41–46, trans. in *Journal of Individual Psychology* (1966), 22, 166–72.

A1928n [Editor with C. Furtmüller and E. Wexberg] *Heilen und Bilden: Ein Buch der Erziehungskunst für Ärzte und Pädagogen* (Healing and educating: a book of the art of education for physicians and educators), 3rd ed. (Munich: Bergmann).

A1929d *The science of living* (New York: Greenberg; as reprinted, Garden City, N.Y.: Doubleday Anchor Books, 1969).

A1930a *The education of children,* trans. Eleanore and F. Jensen (New York: Greenberg; reprinted, Chicago: Henry Regnery, 1970).

A1930d *Das Problem der Homosexualität: erotisches Training und erotischer Rückzug* (The problem of homosexuality: erotic training and erotic retreat), 2nd ed. (Leipzig: Hirzel).

A1930e *Die Technik der Individualpsychologie,* Vol. 2, *Die Seele der schwererziehbaren Schulkinder* (The technique of Individual Psychology, Vol. 2, The soul of difficult schoolchildren) (Munich: Bergmann).

A1930p *Praxis und Theorie der Individualpsychologie* (Practice and theory of Individual Psychology), 4th ed. (Munich: Bergmann).

A1931b *What life should mean to you,* ed. A. Porter (Boston: Little, Brown; reprinted, New York: Putnam Capricorn Books, 1958).

A1933b *Der Sinn des Lebens* (The meaning of life) (Vienna, Leipzig: Passer [trans. A1938a]).

A1938a *Social interest: a challenge to mankind,* trans. J. Linton and R. Vaughan (London: Faber & Faber [orig.: A1933b]; reprinted, New York: Putnam Capricorn Books, 1964).

A1945b The sexual function, *Individual Psychology Bulletin,* 4, 99–102; as reprinted in A1964a, pp. 219–23.

A1956b *The Individual Psychology of Alfred Adler: a systematic presentation in selections from his writings,* ed.

H. L. and Rowena R. Ansbacher (New York: Basic Books; reprinted, New York: Harper & Row, 1964).

A1964a *Superiority and social interest: a collection of later writings,* ed. H. L. and Rowena R. Ansbacher (Evanston, Ill.: Northwestern University Press; reprinted, New York: Norton, 1979).

ADLER'S REFERENCES TO OTHER AUTHORS

Note: For nontechnical authors, and for technical authors where no specific work is mentioned, see the Index.

Aschner, Bernhard. *Die Konstitution der Frau und ihre Beziehungen zur Geburtshilfe und Gynäkologie.* Munich: Bergmann, 1924.

Asnaourow, F. *Sadismus und Masochismus in Kultur und Erziehung.* Munich: Reinhardt, 1913.

Bachofen, Johann J. *Das Mutterrecht: Eine Untersuchung über die Gynekokratie der alten Welt nach ihrer religiösen und rechtlichen Natur.* Stuttgart: Kreis & Hoffmann, 1861 [*Myth, religion, and mother right.* Princeton, N.J.: Princeton University Press, 1967].

Bebel, August. *Die Frau und der Sozialismus.* Stuttgart: Dietz, 1885 [*Woman and socialism.* New York: Socialist Literature Co., 1910].

Birstein, J. Mitteilungen aus der Kinderpsychologie, *Zentralblatt für Psychoanalyse und Psychotherapie* (1913), 4, 81–84.

Bühler, Charlotte. *Seelenleben der Jugendlichen,* 2nd ed. Jena: Fischer, 1923.

Deutsch, Helene. *Psychoanalyse der weiblichen Sexualfunktionen.* Leipzig: Internationaler Psychoanalytischer Verlag, 1925.

Ellis, Havelock. Die Psychologie des normalen Geschlechtstriebes, in A. Moll (ed.), *Handbuch der Sexualwissenschaften.* Leipzig: Vogel, 1912.

Fliess, Wilhelm. *Der Ablauf des Lebens: Grundlegung zur exakten Biologie.* Wien: Deuticke, 1906.

Freud, Sigmund. *Drei Abhandlungen zur Sexualtheorie.*

Wien: Psychoanalytischer Verlag, 1923 [*Three essays on the theory of sexuality*. New York: Basic Books, 1962].

Furtmüller, Carl. *Psychoanalyse und Ethik.* Munich: Reinhardt, 1912.

Hall, G. Stanley. *Adolescence.* New York: Appleton, 1918.

Heymans, G. *Die Psychologie der Frau.* Heidelburg: C. Winter, 1910.

Hirschfeld, Magnus. *Jahrbuch für sexuelle Zwischenstufen.* Stuttgart: Püttmann, n.d.

Hitschmann, Edward. *Freuds Neurosenlehre,* 2nd ed. Leipzig: Deuticke, 1913 [*Freud's theories of the neuroses.* New York: Moffat, Yard, 1917].

Janet, Pierre. *Geisteszustand der Hysterischen.* 1894 [*The mental state of hystericals.* New York: Putnam, 1901].

Jung, Carl G. Die Bedeutung des Vaters für das Schicksal des Einzelnen, *Jahrbuch für psychoanalytische und psychopathologische Forschung,* 1909, 1.

——. *Jahrbuch für psychoanalytische und psychopathologische Forschung,* 1913, 4.

Kant, Immanuel. Anthropologie in pragmatischer Hinsicht (1798), *Gesammelte Schriften,* Vol. 7. Berlin: Reimer, 1917, pp. 117–333.

Key, Ellen. *Über Liebe und Ehe,* 15th ed. Berlin: Fischer, 1911 [*Love and marriage.* New York: Putnam, 1911].

Liepmann, Wilhelm. *Psychologie der Frau,* 2nd ed. Vienna: Urban & Schwarzenberg, 1922.

Mill, John S. *Die Hörigkeit der Frau.* Berlin, 1869 [*The subjection of women.* London: Oxford, 1966].

Möbius, Paul J. *Über den physiologischen Schwachsinn des Weibes,* 5th ed. Halle: Marhold, 1903 [The physiological mental weakness of woman. *Alienist and Neurologist,* 1901, 22, 624–42].

Müller, Robert. *Sexualbiologie.* Berlin: Marcus, 1907.

Rohleder, Hermann. *Die Funktionsstörungen der Zeugung,* 2nd ed.

Schirmacher, Käthe. *Die moderne Frauenbewegung,* 2nd ed. Leipzig: Teubner, 1905 [*The modern woman's rights movement.* New York: Macmillan, 1912].

Sellheim, Hugo. *Das Geheimnis vom Ewig-Weiblichen,* 2nd

ed. Stuttgart: Enke, 1924.
Spranger, Eduard. *Psychologie des Jugendalters,* 4th ed. Leipzig: Quelle & Meyer, 1925.
Tandler, J., and Gross, S. *Die biologischen Grundlagen der sekundären Geschlechtscharaktere.* Berlin: Springer, 1913.
Tumlirz, Otto. *Die Reifejahre.* Leipzig: Klinkhardt, 1924.
Vaerting, M. *Wahrheit und Irrtum in der Geschlechterpsychologie.* Karlsruhe: Braun, 1923.
Vaihinger, H. *Die Philosophie des als ob.* Leipzig: Felix Meiner, 1911 [*The philosophy of "as if."* London: Routledge & Kegan Paul, 1924].
Weininger, Otto. *Geschlecht und Charakter,* 17th ed. Wien: Braumüller, 1918 [*Sex and character.* London: Heinemann, 1906].
Wexberg, Erwin. Rousseau und die Ethik, in A. Adler and C. Furtmüller (eds.), *Heilen und Bilden.* Munich: Reinhardt, 1914, pp. 187–206.
Witt, Alexander. Ein Beitrag zum Thema "Sexuelle Eindrücke beim Kinde," *Zentralblatt für Psychoanalyse und Psychotherapie,* 1911, 1(4), 165–66.

EDITORS' REFERENCES TO OTHER AUTHORS

Adler, K. A. Power in Adlerian Theory, in J. H. Masserman (ed.), *Science and psychoanalysis,* Vol. 20. *The dynamics of power.* New York: Grune & Stratton, 1972, pp. 53–63.
Adler, V. Bemerkungen über die soziologischen Grundlagen des "männlichen Protests" (Comments on the sociological foundations of the "masculine protest"), *Internationale Zeitschrift für Individualpsychologie,* 1925, 3, 307–10.
Ansbacher, H. L. Rudolph Hildebrand: a forerunner of Alfred Adler, *Journal of Individual Psychology,* 1962, 18, 12–17.
——. Sensus privatus versus sensus communis, *Journal of Individual Psychology,* 1965, 21, 48–50.

——. Life style: a historical and systematic review, *Journal of Individual Psychology*, 1967, 23, 191–212.
——. The concept of social interest, *Journal of Individual Psychology*, 1968, 24, 131–49.
——. Adler's interpretation of early recollections: historical account, *Journal of Individual Psychology*, 1973, 29, 135–45.
Bashkirtseva, M. *The journal of a young artist, 1860–1884*, trans. Mary J. Serrano. New York: Cassell & Company, 1889.
Beecher, W. Every stick has two ends, *Individual Psychology Bulletin*, 1946, 5, 84–86.
Bonsal, S. The end of the strange career of "the red countess," New York *Times Magazine*, Oct. 8, 1911, p. 1.
Dolliver, R. H. Alfred Adler and the dialectic, *Journal of the History of the Behavioral Sciences*, 1974, 10, 16–20.
Ellenberger, H. F. *The discovery of the unconscious: the history and evolution of dynamic psychiatry*. New York: Basic Books, 1970.
Freud, S. *Three essays on the theory of sexuality* (1905), trans. and newly ed. J. Strachey. New York: Basic Books, 1962.
——. Psychoanalytic notes upon an autobiographical account of a case of paranoia (dementia paranoides) (1911), in *Collected Papers*, Vol. 3. London: Hogarth, 1925, pp. 385–470.
——. On narcissism: an introduction (1914), in *Standard Edition*, Vol. 14. London: Hogarth, 1957, pp. 67–102. (b)
——. Contributions to the psychology of love. The taboo of virginity (1918), in *Collected Papers*, Vol. 4. London: Hogarth, 1925, pp. 217–35.
——. *The ego and the id* (1923). New York: Norton, 1962.
——. Analysis terminable and interminable (1937), in *Collected Papers*, Vol. 5. London: Hogarth, 1950, pp. 316–57.
Kaufmann, W. *Nietzsche: philosopher, psychologist, Antichrist*, 4th ed. Princeton, N.J.: Princeton University Press, 1974.

Kelly, G. A. *The psychology of personal constructs,* Vol. 1. New York: Norton, 1955.

——. Nonparametric factor analysis of personality theories, *Journal of Individual Psychology,* 1963, 19, 115–47.

Lindsey, B. B., and Evans, W. *The companionate marriage.* New York: Boni & Liveright, 1927.

Money, J., and Ehrhardt, A. A. *Man and woman, boy and girl: the differentiation and dimorphism of gender identity from conception to maturity.* Baltimore: Johns Hopkins University Press, 1972.

Nietzsche, F. Thus spoke Zarathustra: third part (1884), in *The Portable Nietzsche,* ed. Walter Kaufmann. New York: Viking Press, 1968, pp. 260–343.

Nunberg, H., and Federn, E. (eds.). *Minutes of the Vienna Psychoanalytic Society.* New York: International Universities Press, Vol. 1, 1906–8, 1962; Vol. 2, 1908–10, 1967; Vol. 3, 1910–11, 1974.

Powers, R. L. Myth and memory, in H. H. Mosak (ed.), *Alfred Adler: his influence on psychology today.* Park Ridge, N.J.: Noyes Press, 1973, pp. 271–90.

Racowitza, H. *Princess Helene von Racowitza: an autobiography.* New York: Macmillan, 1910.

Rasey, M. J. *Toward maturity: the psychology of child development.* New York: Hinds, Hayden & Eldridge, 1947.

——. *It takes time: an autobiography of the teaching profession.* New York: Harper & Bros., 1953.

Roazen, P. *Freud and his followers.* New York: Knopf, 1975.

Rychlak, J. R. *A philosophy of science for personality theory.* Boston: Houghton Mifflin, 1968.

——. *Introduction to personality and psychotherapy: a theory-construction approach.* Boston: Houghton Mifflin, 1973.

Thilly, F., and Wood, L. *A history of philosophy,* 3rd ed. New York: Holt, Rinehart & Winston, 1957.

Vaihinger, H. *Die Philosophie des als ob: System der theoretischen, praktischen und religiösen Fiktionen der Menschheit auf Grund eines idealistischen Positivismus* (1911) (The philosophy of "as if": A system of the theoretical, practical, and religious fictions of mankind based on an idealistic positivism), 3rd ed. Leipzig: Felix Meiner, 1918. This reference for passages not included in the English edition. (a)

——. *The philosophy of 'as if': a system of the theoretical, practical, and religious fictions of mankind* (1911), trans. C. K. Ogden. London: Routledge & Kegan Paul, 1924. (b)

Vleeschauwer, H. J. de. Kantianism, in Encyclopaedia Britannica, Macropaedia, 1974, Vol. 10, pp. 395–98.

INDEX